Cambridge Elements ≡

Elements in Histories of Emotions and the Senses
edited by
Jan Plamper
University of Limerick

SENSORY PERCEPTION, HISTORY AND GEOLOGY

The Afterlife of Molyneux's Question in British, American and Australian Landscape Painting and Cultural Thought

Richard Read
UWA School of Design

CAMBRIDGE
UNIVERSITY PRESS

CAMBRIDGE
UNIVERSITY PRESS

University Printing House, Cambridge CB2 8BS, United Kingdom

One Liberty Plaza, 20th Floor, New York, NY 10006, USA

477 Williamstown Road, Port Melbourne, VIC 3207, Australia

314–321, 3rd Floor, Plot 3, Splendor Forum, Jasola District Centre, New Delhi – 110025, India

103 Penang Road, #05–06/07, Visioncrest Commercial, Singapore 238467

Cambridge University Press is part of the University of Cambridge.

It furthers the University's mission by disseminating knowledge in the pursuit of education, learning, and research at the highest international levels of excellence.

www.cambridge.org
Information on this title: www.cambridge.org/9781009095488
DOI: 10.1017/9781009091800

First published 2022

A catalogue record for this publication is available from the British Library.

ISBN 978-1-009-09548-8 Paperback
ISSN 2632-1068 (online)
ISSN 2632-105X (print)

Sensory Perception, History and Geology

The Afterlife of Molyneux's Question in British, American and Australian Landscape Painting and Cultural Thought

Elements in Histories of Emotions and the Senses

DOI: 10.1017/9781009091800
First published online: January 2022

Richard Read
UWA School of Design

Author for correspondence: Richard Read, richard.read@uwa.edu.au

Abstract: William Molyneux's question to John Locke about whether a blind man restored to sight could name the difference between a cube and a sphere without touching them shaped fundamental conflicts in philosophy, theology and science between empirical and idealist answers that are radically alien to current ways of seeing and feeling but were born of colonizing ambitions whose devastating genocidal and ecocidal consequences intensify today. This Element demonstrates how landscape paintings of unfamiliar terrains required historical and geological subject matter to supply tactile associations for empirical recognition of space, whereas idealism conferred unmediated but no less coercive sensory access. Close visual and verbal analysis using photographs of pictorial sites trace vividly different responses to the question, from those of William Hazlitt and John Ruskin in Britain to those of nineteenth-century authors and artists in the United States and Australia, including Ralph Waldo Emerson, Thomas Cole, William Haseltine, Fitz Henry Lane and Eugene von Guérard.

Keywords: Molyneux's question, colonial landscape painting, verbal/visual enquiry, William Hazlitt, Ralph Waldo Emerson

ISBNs: 9781009095488 (PB), 9781009091800 (OC)
ISSNs: 2632-1068 (online), 2632-105X (print)

Contents

1 Seeing as Painting

The contention of this Element is that confrontations between sight and land-forms, as registered in British, North American and Australian landscape paintings of the late eighteenth and nineteenth centuries, and particularly as influenced by the increasing middle-class enthusiasm for the science of geology, presented an opportunity for speculations upon the means by which nature and human consciousness fit together, with dire implications for who and what was categorized as valuably human or not, as well as for the environment that sustained them. Dominant in these speculations was the increasing competition between theological and scientific explanations of the origins of the planet, in which the histories of the eye and the environment it observes were instrumental in the union or segregation of human and natural history. Of the three components of my title – sensory perception, history and geology – the first refers to the mode in which paintings and their descriptions envision the subject matter of the second and third components and how theories of perception dawned alongside colonial ambitions over many centuries, for it is within the development of technologies of colonialism for exploring and securing previously unconquered, if far from uninhabited, territories that the impact of Molyneux's question on art and culture provides the focus of this Element. It does so in relation to Britain, the United States and Australia, the latter being countries that by the nineteenth century were or had been colonies of the British empire but were also subject to the scientific and cultural influences of other European countries. Molyneux's question serves as a clarifying lens for how philosophy and art might influence each other and together influence the social and political landscape of various places and times, providing novel insight and interconnections to these histories and geographies.

In 1693 the Anglo-Irish philosopher and politician William Molyneux posed to his friend, the philosopher John Locke, the question of whether a blind man newly restored to sight would be able to name the difference between a sphere and a cube without resorting to touch, the only faculty through which he could have prior knowledge of their different solid shapes. It is important to attend carefully to the vividly compressed language Molyneux used to clinch what he called his 'jocose problem' (quoted in Berman 2009, 139):

> *Suppose a Man born blind, and now adult, and taught by his touch to distinguish between a Cube, and a Sphere of the same metal, and nighly of the same bigness, so as to tell, when he felt one and t'other, which is the Cube, which the Sphere. Suppose then the Cube and Sphere placed on a Table, and the Blind Man be made to see. Quaere, Whether by his sight, before he*

touch'd them, he could now distinguish, and tell, which is the Globe, which the Cube. (Molyneux quoted in Locke 1975, 146; his emphasis)

Though Locke did not take this up until the second edition of his *Essay Concerning Human Understanding* (1694), he agreed with Molyneux, as would George Berkeley and many others (Glenney 2013a; for positive answers see Riskin 2002, 25–31), that the newly sighted blind man would be unable to 'tell' – naming is important – a sphere apart from a cube without the aid of touch, for otherwise there must exist an innate, amodal correspondence between the separate ideas of sight and touch that transcends immediate sensory experience of a retinal image presumed flat and so unable to convey the distance, position, mass, shape, texture and magnitude of either object. As an empirical philosopher implacably opposed to innate ideas formed in the Rationalist tradition of René Descartes, Baruch Spinoza and Gottfried Leibniz, Locke could not assent to such a proposition. Rather, he argued that if the newly sighted blind man could not bring his habitual memory of touch to the image on his retina, he would see the sphere only as 'a flat Circle variously shadowed, with several degrees of Light and Brightness ... *as is evident in Painting*' (1975, 145; emphasis added).[1] Molyneux's question became a battleground between key European philosophers about whether empiricism (the epistemology of science) or idealism (innate ideas, rationalism) best explained the mind's access to ideas about the world. I shall argue that Molyneux's question helped to generate models of transformation or preservation of untouched Nature that informed distinctions between the aesthetic categories of the Beautiful, the Sublime and especially the Picturesque.

The analogy between seeing and painting dates back to Johannes Kepler's publication in 1604 of his discovery that sight takes place on the retina, which, though curved, performed a similar role to the canvas in receiving a two-dimensional image through the action of light 'as if it were some tips of small paintbrushes (*apices penicillorum*)' (quoted in Dumitrescu 2017, 50). Kepler decisively tipped the scales in favour of the Aristotelian theory of intromission (sight as the passive reception of light from the outside world) in its ancient battle with the Platonic theory of extromission (in which the eyes emit particles of light that beam objects into the mind). In this Kepler was following the example of 'the artist-architect-engineers' in their objectification of light through the development of optical instruments such as the camera obscura

---

[1] Modern philosophers discriminate more precisely than most earlier readers between the different respects in which Locke thought retinal images were unintelligible. See Walter Ott (2020, 280) for the definition most consistently relevant to nineteenth-century commentators on painting: 'Only touch can prompt ... [Molyneux man] to inflate his two-dimensional image into a visual idea of a three-dimensional shape.'

for the rendering of pictorial perspective (Straker 1976, 7–8). Kepler's use of pictorial language to describe the operations of sight was primarily motivated by his admiration for Albrecht Dürer, who had discovered Renaissance perspective science on a trip to Bologna in 1506 and later codified it (Straker 1976, 12–13). Kepler's concentration on the mechanics of vision had the effect of pushing the soul 'back behind the eye where it resides in severe danger of absolute eviction' (Straker 1976, 21).

Despite claims by the anatomist Galen of Pergamon in the second century BC that sight takes place on the crystalline humour, the belief that the only immediate component of vision is the mental representation of a two-dimensional image belongs to a tradition reaching back to Euclid and Ptolemy in ancient antiquity and was considerably boosted in the twelfth century AD by the Islamic natural philosopher Alhazen, who first argued for a one-to-one match between world and visual experience, which rendered the extromissionist theory untenable (Hatfield 2009, 358–61; Straker 1976, 10). Kepler's analogy between seeing and painting was also prepared by the development of one-point perspective painting in fifteenth-century Italy, which depended on the assumption that the plane section of the picture surface through the cone of sight is an adequate reproduction of the visual image (Panofsky 1991, 28).

These, then, were some of the precedents for what the American psychologist James J. Gibson called

> the classical assumption that two-dimension vision is immediate, primitive or sensory, while three-dimensional vision is secondary derived or perceptual. One must first see a plane form before one can see a solid form. This notion is connected with the argument that the three-dimensional properties of things can have no correlates in a two-dimensional retinal image, and that the three-dimensional properties must therefore be reconstructed by the mind or the brain. (Gibson 1951, 404)

This tradition also raised the question of whether humans are conscious of these flat representations of the three-dimensional world before the mind interprets them as direct experience of that world, a question that could have no meaning until Descartes' strict division in 1641 'between mechanistically conceived physiological processes and sensations in the soul' of which only the latter could be conscious (Hatfield 2009, 372). The consequence of Descartes' division of these two hitherto undifferentiated realms of matter and spirit was to unify Aristotle's separate powers of the mind into a single, rational, conscious entity tantamount to the modern conception of the self (p. 377). This concept was necessary for first-person validation of experience that facilitated disengagement from the world, the better to act on it. Such psychological understanding of perception propelled, into the nineteenth century and beyond, the classical assumption that painting might be a more immediate representation of vision than experience of actuality itself (p. 384). It is the distance of these assumptions from our own experience of perception (see **Section 10**) that endows the sensory and emotional configurations discussed in this Element with radical alterity.

Three stages of perception may be assumed in this long tradition of perception: first, the non-conscious retinal image; then, from Descartes and Berkeley onwards, two conscious stages, a mental idea of the retinal image of which we are only fleetingly aware, followed by a stage in which the mind acts on tactile memories to turn flat mental representations into seemingly immediate experiences of a fully three-dimensional world (Hatfield 2009, 358, 376). For those in the grip of this tradition, the process of perception is mirrored by the spectator's resolution of a flat painting into an illusion of the outside world and by the art critic's description of it – for Molyneux's question, we remember, entailed naming as well as perceiving.

Quaint as Molyneux's succinct language seems now, it bears out W. K. Wimsatt Jr's verdict that, like other thought experiments characteristic of seventeenth-century empirical science, Molyneux's question was one 'which almost anybody might be expected to understand' and 'many might be expected to emulate', since its diction 'had an average generality and easiness of meaning' (Wimsatt 1948, 10) that gave it wide appeal, especially at a time when scientific experiments were taking over from philosophical ratiocination in finding answers to fundamental questions. The 'multifarious or indeterminate' relations between speculative and experimental philosophy became hard to disentangle in the nineteenth century (Anstey and Vanzo 2019, 2), though some thinkers, such as Ralph Waldo Emerson, would always resist Samuel Taylor Coleridge's successful insistence in 1833 on protecting the term 'philosopher' from contamination by the term 'scientist' (Walls 2003, 62–3).

While Enlightenment philosophers from Locke to Kant endeavoured to clear space for the validation of empirical science within theories of mind, Locke's insistence, following Aristotle, that nothing is in the intellect that was not first in the senses and that complex ideas derive from simple ideas based on sense impressions raised the crucial problem of how to preserve operations of the mind from a purely passive, mechanistic response to sensations (Locke 1975, 158). If the mind is not granted innate powers a priori before external reality floods it a posteriori through the senses, how can it attend to what, in the undifferentiated, chaotic scheme of sensations, answers its needs and inclinations through the passions? This had been the premise on which Leibniz built his rationalist qualification to the Aristotelian and Thomist dictum that 'nothing is in the intellect which was not first in sense' with the devastating addition (Cassirer 1951, 99) 'nisi ipse intellectus' – except the intellect itself (Leibniz 1981, 111). Not just the content but also the energies of mind needed accounting for (Cassirer 1951, 127), and on this depended the issue of whether the ego and the world belonged to the different strata of spirit and perceived reality (Descartes), on a continuously materialist or continuously spiritual spectrum between them (Locke and Berkeley, respectively), or on a middle course between innate ideas and empirical impressions, which Immanuel Kant took to fit the inner and outer worlds together (Scruton 2001, 30, 53).

The difficulty of aligning the mind with the world explains why Molyneux's question became the 'common centre' of 'all the special problems of eighteenth-century epistemology and psychology' (Cassirer 1951, 108) and 'the key issue in the debate between innate ideas and sensory experience' (Paterson 2006, 7). This is because it asked whether sensory perception is specific to each sensory modality as a unique portal to the world or whether it is amodal and so reliant on innate ideas to establish transfers of knowledge across sense modalities. Since art was both an instance and a metaphor of the various ways mind and world correspond to each other, the appeal of Molyneux's question to artists and critics lay in its dramatic role as an axle on which the weightiest alternative conceptions of the truth might turn. For William Hazlitt, whose writings are the subject of the next three sections, 'the arts of painting and poetry are conversant with the world of thought within us, and with the world of sense without us – with what we know, and see, and feel intimately' (Hazlitt 1930–4, vol. 18, 9). As a framing device, the stark sensory duality of Molyneux's question may itself have inspired the wide variety of emotional responses expressed in the art and thought considered in this Element.

2 Hazlitt on Wilson

The centrality of Molyneux's question emerges in the British Romantic essayist William Hazlitt's response to landscape paintings by Richard Wilson, Aelbert Cuyp and Nicolas Poussin, artists who each called on different regimes of sensory perception and emotional affect from his sophisticated philosophical armoury.[2] In his brilliant but ambivalent review 'Wilson's Landscapes, at the British Institution' in *The Champion* newspaper of 17 July 1814, he awarded laurels to *Apollo* (c18; **Figure 1**) and *Phaeton* (c18), two of Wilson's Italianate landscapes in the manner of Claude Lorraine. Hazlitt reads them as companion

---

[2] Indeed, other respondents discussed in this Element used different readings of Molyneux's question without rigorous consistency, but, with the possible exception of Denis Diderot (Morgan 1977, 28), none of them consciously approached it as a comprehensive 'cluster concept of disjunctive sub-problems' as a modern philosopher might do (Glenney 2013b, 542).

Figure 1 Richard Wilson, *Apollo and the Seasons* (c18), oil on canvas, 100.1 × 125.7 cm, Fitzwilliam Museum, University of Cambridge, United Kingdom

pieces that capture the transition between a spring morning and an autumnal evening in ancient antiquity:

> In looking at them we breath [sic] the very air which the scene inspires, and feel the genius of the place present to us. In the first, there is all the cool freshness of a misty spring morning: the sky, the water, the dim horizon all convey the same feeling. The fine grey tone, and varying outline of the hills, the graceful form of the retiring lake, broken still more by the hazy shadows of the objects that repose on its bosom; the light trees that expand their branches in the air, and the dark stone figures and mouldering temple, that contrast strongly with the broad clear light of the rising day, give a charm, a truth, a force and harmony to this landscape, which produce the greater pleasure the longer it is dwelt on. – The distribution of light and shade resembles the effect of light on a globe.
>
> The *Phaeton* has the dazzling fervid appearance of an autumnal evening; the golden radiance streams in solid masses from behind the flickering clouds; every object is baked in the sun; – the brown foreground, the thick foliage of the trees, the streams shrunk and stealing along behind the dark high banks, combine to produce that richness, and characteristic propriety of effect, which is to be found only in nature, or in art derived from the study and imitation of nature. The glowing splendour of this landscape reminds us of

the saying of Wilson, that in painting such subjects, he endeavoured to give the effect of insects dancing in the evening sun. His eye seemed formed to drink in the light. These two pictures, as they have the greatest general effect, are also more carefully finished in the particular details than the other pictures in the collection. This circumstance may be worth the attention of those who are apt to think that strength and slovenliness are the same thing.

(Hazlitt 1814b, vol. 18, 24–5)

These intense, extended descriptions conclude with a dig at the president of the Royal Society, Sir Joshua Reynolds, whose theory of abstraction required general forms in art to be purged of the accidental details and defects of nature. Hazlitt commits to an opposing theory of art in which 'the details and peculiarities of nature are only inconsistent with abstract ideas, and not with general or aggregate effects' (Hazlitt 1930–4, vol. 18, 77).

Although Lessing had claimed in the *Laocoön* (1766) that a picture can only represent static scenes, here in *Apollo* we perceive the trees growing, the stones mouldering and the day rising; and, in *Phaeton*, the evening sun streaming and the stream stealing through a landscape that has been 'baked'. At the same time, objects break down into finer detail as they absorb our attention: 'the retiring lake, *broken still more* by the hazy shadows' (emphasis added). These are of course the artist's as well as the spectator's observations. We notice, therefore, a subtle combination of vocabularies from nature and painting (the 'tone' and 'outline' of the 'hills', the 'graceful form' of the 'lake') whereby our awareness of the painting and the landscape alternates and merges. The description refers sometimes to particular objects in the landscapes – 'dark stone figure' and 'thick foliage' – and sometimes to the material properties of the paint: 'radiance' is only 'solid' when painted. There is certainly no attempt to keep subject, image and description apart (Hazlitt 1814b, vol. 18, 24–5). Rather, their distinctions are suspended to forge an identity between natural processes, artistic technique, sensory perception and subjective feeling that compresses the contrasting moments from a spring morning and autumnal evening from another age into an experience of successive perceptions in an art gallery.

Emulating the poetry of James Thomson's *Seasons*, Hazlitt's syntax re-enacts excursions of the eye over diagonals linking variegated bands of landscape scenery to the bright horizon where it rebounds upon tonal contrast to the foreground (Barrell 1972, 6–34). In the *Apollo* it wanders back to the foreground but rebounds from the dark temple there to the 'clear light of day' at the horizon, a movement prompted by abrupt tonal contrasts. But after the varied pace of movement between the horizon and the foreground in each picture, the eye finally comes to rest on the overall 'effects of insects dancing in the sun' (Hazlitt 1814b, vol. 18, 24–5). The general effect and uniform feeling of each picture repose on the overall impression of this aggregated mass of shifting detail.

Fusion of detail with space is fundamental to a further quality of Hazlitt's descriptive style, which is deeply implicated in amodal or intermodal schemes of sense perception: the delicately controlled literary synaesthesia that plays about Wilson's scenes, as in 'the cool freshness of a misty morning' (Hazlitt 1814b, vol. 18, 25). Literary synaesthesia allows Hazlitt to establish imaginary parallels between nature, painting, sensation and feeling that determine the sort of detail that is fixed yet 'dancing', single yet 'blended'. It entails an ambiguity registered in the alternative words Hazlitt elsewhere uses to define: '*gusto* or expression: *i.e.* the conveying to the eye the impressions of the soul, *or* the other senses connected with the sense of sight' (Hazlitt 1830–4, vol. 18, 106; his emphases). Apart from the usual sense of zest or relish that 'gusto' still conveys today, these alternative roles for the senses and the soul signal a weighty philosophical conundrum that persists in his definition in the essay 'On *Gusto*': 'In a word, gusto in painting is where the impression made on one sense excites by affinity those of another' (Hazlitt 1816, vol. 4, 78). Thus, in claiming that 'we breath the very air which the scene inspires', the play on breathing and inspiration raises the question of 'how far such language is merely metaphorical, or how far it signifies an actual excitation of the senses' (Chase 1924, 196), known today as the relatively rare physical condition of true synaesthesia. Thus he sometimes concedes that he is writing fancifully to convey 'the force and precision of individual details, transferred, *as it were*, to the page from the canvas' (Hazlitt 1930–4, vol. 11, 166; emphasis added) but at other times would have us believe that our senses really do integrate with each other to penetrate the picture's surface to some indisputable reality in nature past or present on which even the most imaginative history paintings depend for their conviction (Hazlitt 1930–4, vol. 18, 78).

Hazlitt's earliest philosophical writings attest to a polarity between matter and operations of mind that underlie the dynamic interaction between feeling, painting and nature in Wilson's synaesthetic effects: 'it might be said . . . that we have one source of ideas, *viz.* sensation, and another source of ideas, *viz.* ideas', he writes in *Lectures on English Philosophy* (Hazlitt 1812, vol. 2, 149). Hazlitt confusedly takes this dualism from Immanuel Kant, for, hampered by a bad translation (Welleck 1931, 165–71), he failed to grasp that Kant resolved the conflicting strata of the ego and the world with a transcendental deduction in which 'a priori knowledge provides support for, but it also derives its content from, empirical discovery' (Scruton 2001, 30). Kant held that the limitations of personal experience and individual point of view denied consciousness access to a priori, timeless, spaceless knowledge of supersensuous reality that Leibniz thought available. Hazlitt's failure to understand this limitation led him on an erratic course between Locke's empirical theory that the mind is passive before reality and Bishop Berkeley's theory that only the mind exists. Meanwhile, he could not countenance the lapse into solipsism that David Hume's extreme empiricism entailed, wherein, as Hazlitt put it, 'each separate impression must remain absolutely simple and distinct, unknown to and unconscious of the rest, shut up in the narrow cell of its own individuality' (Hazlitt 1930–4, vol. 20, 25).

Using his imperfect knowledge of Kant as a guide between this Scylla and Charybdis in both his philosophical writings and art criticism, Hazlitt some-times appears to desert Kant for either Berkeley or Locke. Kant persuades him that there is no significance in the material realm without the action of the perceiving mind: *'the mind alone is formative*, to use the expression of a great German writer . . . There is no object or idea which does not consist of a number of parts arranged in a certain manner, but of this arrangement the parts them-selves cannot be sensible' (Hazlitt 1812, vol. 2, 153; his emphasis). The important implication for his art criticism is that form, though potentially in matter, is realized only when the mind reassembles the particles of matter into wholes. Therefore his descriptions of the mind abound with attributions of form, not as something static but with the qualities of a gerund: the mind is 'a superintending faculty, which alone perceives the relations of things, and enables us to comprehend their connexions, forms and masses' (Hazlitt 1930–4, vol. 20, 25); it is a 'surrounding and forming power' (Hazlitt 1812, vol. 2: 151), a 'cementing power' and without it 'All nature, all objects, all parts of objects would be equally "without form and void"' (Hazlitt 1930–4, vol. 2, 152–3). But if form exists only in the mind, then the importance of matter quickly recedes, for are we not the cause of the form that affects us in matter?

In fact, Hazlitt argues vehemently in his philosophy and criticism that the complex qualities perceptible in objects actually inhere in them as raw materials or potential ideas for the 'forms or moulds' of the mind to activate (1812, vol. 2, 166). Art seems particularly suited to the moulds of the mind so has special power to generate ideas of the world it refers to. Hence the importance of technique. Wilson's brushstrokes allow our pleasure to grow with the growing of the trees. It is the continuity of style between *Apollo* and *Phaeton* that turns the morning and the evening of each picture into related moments. In these moments, optical movements and teeming detail are synaesthetically united by a consciousness that the critic re-enacts for the bourgeois body of the growing reading public who attend the new public art galleries (see **Section 4**).

Yet the problem remains: we still do not know how qualities belong both to objects and to our perceptions of them, whether these qualities are mental or material, or how they coincide in perception. His belief in a dialectical relationship between the details of matter and the shaping power of the mind lacks philosophical rigour due to incompatible allegiances. 'Revoking epistemology, yet tied by habit and tradition to empiricism's demand for at least some criterion of truth, Hazlitt's thought is suspended between the imperative for a proper account of knowledge, and the obvious attraction of a theory of human psychological activity based upon the paradigm of intellectual energy' (Milnes 2000, 5). The dilemma erupts in a crucial sentence linking the descriptions of *Phaeton* and *Apollo* but also cut off from them by a dash: '– The distribution of light and shade resembles the effect of light on a globe' (Hazlitt 1814b, vol. 18, 24). To what does this analogy refer in a painting in which there is nothing globe-like?

One possibility is that Hazlitt is referring to the terrestrial globe that was a common feature of British intellectual life in Georgian interiors. As such it reverses the contraction of scale observed in 'On Going a Journey', where he uses a terrestrial globe to show how lived experience dwarfs abstract understanding: 'What is the true signification of that immense mass of territory and population, known by the name of China to us? An inch of paste-board on a wooden globe, of no more account than a china orange! Things near us are seen of the size of life: things at a distance are diminished to the size of the understanding' (1822a, vol. 8, 187). Throughout this Element we will encounter other contractions and expansions of consciousness. A mismatch between the microworld and the world of knowledge was inherent in William Gilpin's theologically grounded theory of the picturesque where the sketcher excises the details and combines the forms of natural scenes to facilitate their approximation to art works, which are but inferior reflections of nature's overall perfection as God would see it: 'She works on a *vast scale*; and, no doubt, harmoniously, if her scheme could be comprehended. The artist in the mean time is confined to a *span*' (1782, 18; his emphases). Hazlitt's globe analogy, however, works in the opposite way. Rather than transcending the spectator's limited scope, it draws the world into its range. It endows Wilson's Arcadian scenes with a macrocosmic scale and global amplitude that anticipates Ralph Waldo Emerson's claim that 'a work of art' is 'an epitome of the world' (1836, vol. 1, 23). Likewise, in perfecting the Romantic essay form, Hazlitt draws the boundless realm of contemporary empirical knowledge into the aesthetic intensity of personal experience where he seeks to evoke human experience as a whole (Milnes 2019).

An alternative to this macrocosmic explanation is that the analogy, which bears no relation to the painting, illuminates the internal operations of sensory perception by recalling the globe in Molyneux's question. Either the haste of a busy journalist or common knowledge of the cube and sphere experiment may explain the brevity of Hazlitt's allusion, but in his *Lectures on English Philosophy* delivered two years earlier he had quoted the figure of the globe from the very passage on Molyneux's question in Locke's *An Essay Concerning Human Understanding* where, as we saw already, the formation of retinal impressions is likened to painting (Hazlitt 1812, vol. 2, 182). If we take Hazlitt's passing reference to the globe as an allusion to this controversy, a tight fit emerges with the descriptions, for it provides the critic with an opportunity to re-enact a universal model of sensory perception through the evaluative interpretation of a specific painting, for art criticism is a form of epideictic, the rhetoric of praise and blame. For the painter, the manipulations of brushes and pencils vicariously re-enacts proprioception, the bodily motility of our earliest negotiations with the world, for 'by the aid of the pencil we may be said to touch and handle the objects of sight' (Hazlitt 1930–4, vol. 8, 7). Thus, in a painting by Claude (or these by Wilson), 'the eye wanders at liberty under the open sky, explores distant objects, and returns back as from a delightful journey' (Hazlitt 1814b, vol. 18, 28). For the reader, Hazlitt's synaesthesia re-enacts the habitual associations of flat retinal images with memories of touch, taste, smell and movement to substantiate the multisensorial reality of a painting that is absent in the same way that a morning in ancient Greece was absent from the spectator-artist or a globe from someone who has never touched one. However, the issue then arises as to whether Hazlitt's evocation implicitly gives a negative answer to the question, as Locke had, or a positive one, as (with the exception of Berkeley, explained in **Section 3**) an idealist would.

   Hazlitt had issued two characteristically astute challenges in the *Lectures* to Locke's negative answer. Firstly, if there is no resemblance between tactile and visual sensations, why should the sensations of either faculty resemble anything in the external world, when such resemblance is essential to Locke's principle that knowledge reaches the intellect only through the senses? Hazlitt's second challenge argues for conceptual communality between heterogeneous senses: 'the mind must recognize a certain similarity between the impressions of different senses in this case. For instance, the sudden change or discontinuity of the sensation, produced by the sharp angles of the cube, is something common to other ideas, and if so, must afford a means of comparing them together' (Hazlitt 1812, vol. 2, 184). This argument reformulates the positive answer given by Molyneux's contemporary Edward Synge, by Leibniz in the eighteenth century (Glenney 2013a) and by Hazlitt's friend John Fearn, a disciple of Kant who had asserted that '*all* our *external Senses* do, more or *less*, betray Extension, sufficiently to prove this [synaesthetic] sort of analogy between them' (Fearn 1812, 57; his emphases). In the perfect reciprocity between aesthetic technique, synaesthetic effect and the unfolding of depth in the descriptions of *Apollo* and *Phaeton*, it seems that Hazlitt again inclines towards a positive answer. On this occasion it is based on Kant's idealist conviction that we grasp the relation of our faculties to the world through the aesthetic experience of nature (Scruton 2001, 99).

Rather alarmingly, the rest of Hazlitt's review abandons this favourable impression of unmediated, multisensory access to depth, for only the illusions of Wilson's Italianate paintings are found spatially convincing. It seems that Wilson fails when tackling unfamiliar subject matter, such as the comparatively novel destinations on the alternative grand tour of Britain, occasioned by the closure of Europe due to the Napoleonic Wars (1803–15). His depictions of Cumberland, Westmoreland and Wales, for example (**Figure 2**), are found wanting, for they lacked the time-honoured associations of the Roman Campagna suggested by the paintings of Claude and Nicolas Poussin. Even if the spectator had visited these unfamiliar locations, his paintings of them hold no more conviction than a map of China on a paste-board globe. Hazlitt is deeply moved by the wild sublimity of such places, yet the interior realms of feeling they animate fits them for poetry rather than painting, despite the

Figure 2 Richard Wilson, *Snowdon from Llyn Nantle*, c.1765–6, oil on canvas, 101 × 127 cm, Lady Lever Art Gallery, Liverpool

strenuous muscular effort of exploring them that we might have expected to substantiate their spatiality for him.

> However stupendous the scenery of that country is, and however powerful and lasting the impression it must always make on the imagination, yet the effect is not produced merely through the eye of the spectator, it arises chiefly from collateral and associated feelings. There is the knowledge of the distance from which we have seen the objects, in the midst of which we are now placed, – the slow, improgressive motion which we make in traversing them, – the abrupt precipice, – the torrent's roar, – the dizzy rapture and boundless expanse of the prospect from the highest mountains, – the difficulty of their ascent, – their loneliness, and silence; – in short, there is a constant sense and superstitious awe of the collective power of matter, of the gigantic and eternal forms of nature, on which from the beginning of time the hand of man has made no impression, and which by the lofty reflections they excite in him, give a sort of intellectual sublimity even to his sense of physical weakness. (Hazlitt 1814b, vol. 18, 26)

Many of these phrases are lifted directly from Hazlitt's 'Observations on Mr. Wordsworth's Poem The Excursion' (1814a, vol. 4, 111–12). Their breathless, disjointed impressions, broken off by dashes to prevent them from forming the syntactical whole and spatial geometry of the *Apollo* and *Phaeton* descriptions, lead to 'lofty impressions' characteristic of Wordsworth's epiphanies in similar mountains terrains in the Lake District and at Mount Snowden. The succession of harsh sensations modulates into generalized spiritual intuitions reminiscent of 'Tintern Abbey': 'A motion and a spirit, that impels / All thinking things, all objects of all thought, / And rolls through all things' (Wordsworth 1961, 63). But this incoherent onrush of non-visual associations leaves no doubt that Hazlitt is progressively abandoning the initial visual impression of wilderness 'on which from the beginning of time the hand of man has made no impression' in order to perform poetically what Archibald Alison had stated prosaically towards the beginning of his associationist polemic *Essays on the Nature and Principles of Taste* (1790):

> Thus, when we feel either the beauty or sublimity of natural scenery ... we are conscious of a variety of images in our mind, very different from those the objects themselves can present to the eye. Trains of pleasing or of solemn thought arise spontaneously within our minds; our hearts swell with emotions, of which the objects before us seem to afford no adequate cause; and we are never so much satiated with delight, as when, in recalling our attention, we are unable to trace either the progress or the connection of those thoughts, which have passed with so much rapidity through our imagination.
>
> (Alison 1790, 2–3)

Joseph Addison, too, contributes to the decoupling of Hazlitt's imaginative associations from the initial visual impression: 'The pleasure of these secondary views of the imagination are of a wider and more universal nature than those it has when joined with sight' (Addison 1710, vol. 5, 3). 'Secondary', here, resembles Hazlitt's 'collateral and associated feelings', and both are related to Locke's 'secondary qualities', which do not inhere in external objects (Hazlitt 1812, vol. 2, 170). Locke and Gilpin combine initial impressions then arrest them as complex ideas and images (Locke 1975, 178; Gilpin 1794, 50), whereas Alison sacrifices the initial impression to a flow of associations driven by the imagination, as Hazlitt does here. Such sequences of association comport well with Edmund Burke's category of the sublime, which overwhelms the senses, but Hazlitt denies them to the picturesque, whose meaning he seems to subvert into the merely picturable:

> There is little in all these circumstances that can be translated into the picturesque, which depends not on the objects themselves, so much as on the symmetry and relation of these objects to one another. In a picture a mountain shrinks to a molehill, and the lake that expands its broad bosom to the sky, seems hardly big enough to launch a fleet of cockle-shells.
>
> (Hazlitt 1930–4, vol. 18, 26)

Unrelieved by tactile memories, flatness creates a sensory impasse, a reduction to Locke's 'flat circle, variously shadowed' (Locke 1975, p. 145) instead of a globe solidified by culturally enhanced memories. As Gilpin nominated '*roughness*' as a tactile criterion of picturesque effect (1794, 6; his italics), so Hazlitt required a kind of optical pinball game for paintings to qualify as picturesque. As he elsewhere argued: 'To be a subject for painting, a prospect must present sharp striking points of view or singular forms, or one object must relieve and set off another. There must be distinct stages and salient points for the eye to rest upon or start from, in its progress over the expanse before it' (Hazlitt 1930–4, vol. 8, 318; his emphasis).

But more than optical mechanisms are at stake in the souring of Hazlitt's opinion of Wilson. There is a sense in which Hazlitt seems to disqualify painting in general rather than British scenery in particular when it comes to finding spatial amplitude for novel subjects. The picturesque movement intensified visual attention to nature, and for Gilpin 'the love of novelty' was an important way of piquing the amusement of sketching (1794, 48). But Gilpin imposed strict limits on the decorum of such interest. His 'picturesque eye' for Irish scenery, for example, was more attracted to the abiding interest of the lake of Killarney than to the eccentric novelty of the Giant Causeway, and, like Hazlitt, Gilpin's emotional preference was ultimately for the '*most usual* forms' of nature (p. 43; his emphasis). Likewise, Hazlitt's review finally establishes Wilson's inferiority to the older artist. Though it is nominally Claude's greater grasp of authentic detail within the unity of his paintings that subordinates Wilson (the attack on Reynolds' general forms again), Claude commands mastery of space largely because the space he commands is enshrined in the prestigious cultural memory of Italian classicism. The very criterion of innovative, imaginative empathy based on cosmopolitan tradition contains the seeds of a Eurocentric anti-colonial bias whose internalized mirror image is the rejection of British regionalism, except where Romantic poetry is concerned.

3 Hazlitt on Cuyp

Hazlitt was aware that Molyneux's question was taken up and developed as the central point of Bishop Berkeley's *New Theory of Vision* (1709), a work that 'has remained, almost from its first promulgation, one of the least disputed doctrines in that most disputed and most disputable of all sciences, – the science of man' (Pastore 1971, 71–2). But in seeming to endorse Locke's answer to Molyneux's question, Berkeley was entirely misunderstood by generations of commentators, for the *New Theory of Vision* was the prolegomenon to his *Principles of Human Knowledge*, published one year later, which rejects matter and a material universe in its entirety. Though preserving a direct connection between a real world and the sense of touch in the earlier work (Riskin 2002, 28), by pursuing empirical ideas of tactile and visual association to the point of collapse Berkeley was preparing an account in the later work of consciousness supplied by God instead of the external world. While Locke's goal was to disprove the existence of innate complex *sensations*, Berkeley's was to disprove the existence of unitary *objects* of sensation. He trenchantly maintained, therefore, that ideas of sight and touch, though habitually associated, have nothing in common either with each other or with a corporeal, external world. Strictly speaking, therefore, distance and distant objects are invisible (Morgan 1977, 59–105). By ensuring commensurability between tactile and visual sensations that otherwise bore no relation to each other, he collapses empiricism into idealism (direct knowledge can only be had of ideas) and immateralism (metaphysical denial of the material world), leaving God alone to vouchsafe stable recognition of a world from which the intermediary role of solid matter is excised.

Though he admired the power Berkeley accorded the mind, the commonsensical Hazlitt was no more convinced by Berkeley's position in the *Principles* that 'all those bodies which compose the mighty frame of the world, have not any subsistence without a mind' (quoted in Hazlitt 1812, vol. 2, 175) than he could accept Hume's sceptical hypothesis of a mind 'shut up in the narrow cell of its own individuality' (p. 152). Yet where Aelbert Cuyp's *Herdsmen with Cows* was concerned, in 'The Dulwich Gallery' (Hazlitt 1823) he playfully entertained the idea of Berkeley's theory as a spur to the imagination (**Figure 3**):

> A fine gallery of pictures is a sort of illustration of Berkeley's Theory of Matter and Spirit. It is like a palace of thought – another universe, built of air, of shadows, of colours. Every thing seems 'palpable to feeling as to sight'. Substances turn to shadows by the painter's arch-chemic touch; shadows harden into substances. 'The eye is made the fool of the other senses, or else worth all the rest.' The material is in some sense embodied in the immaterial, or, at least, we see all things in a sort of intellectual mirror. The world of art is an enchanting deception. We discover distance in a glazed surface; a province is contained in a foot of canvass, a thin evanescent tint gives the form and pressure of rocks and trees; an inert shape has life and motion in it. Look at the Cuyp next door . . . It is woven of ethereal hues. A soft mist is on it, a veil of subtle air. The tender green of the vallies [sic] beyond the gleaming lake, the purple light of the hills, have an effect like the down on an unripe nectarine. You may lay your finger on the canvass; but miles of dewy vapour and sunshine are between you and the object you survey. (Hazlitt 1823, vol. 10, 19)

To call a gallery of pictures a 'sort of illustration' of Berkeley's immaterialism is to equivocate between the sense of a philosophy exemplified and

Figure 3 Aelbert Cuyp, *Herdsmen with Cows*, c.1645, oil on canvas, 101.4 × 145.8 cm, DPG128, Dulwich Picture Gallery, London

a falsehood visualized: how things would look if Berkeley's theory were true when it is not. At first Hazlitt seems to intend the second, for he did not believe that reality is 'another universe, built of air'. Berkeley's theory simply shifts the mind into another register, like the adjuration to move from listening to the author to 'look at the Cuyp next door', or like the strikingly irrelevant analogy with 'an effect like the down on an unripe nectarine'. As he explained elsewhere: 'For description in words (to produce any vivid impression) requires a translation of the object into some other form, which is the language of metaphor and the imagination' (Hazlitt 1930–4, vol. 20, 305). The nectarine image is as obtrusive as the analogy between Wilson's *Apollo* and the globe but serves the opposite purpose. There it established an illusion of reality; here it evokes the reality of an illusion. The globe enlarged and solidified the illusions of space, whereas the nectarine scatters and confuses taste, touch and vision even as it establishes parallels between painterly, retinal and verbal veils through which imaginative memory reifies illusion. The nectarine slips into the reader's mind with the hypnogogic force of déjà vu, like one of those childhood memories 'all spruce, voluptuous and fine' that Hazlitt pondered in 'Why Distant Objects Please' (1822b, vol. 8, 257).

Childhood, it transpires, is a generative trope that fosters movement between ontological realms in the chapter's narrative structure. In the vivid autumnal scene at the beginning of the chapter, Hazlitt contemplates the cycle of the seasons as 'Winter gently let go the hand of Summer' (1823, vol. 10, 17). Seasonal change anticipates the looping generations of schoolboys of whom he singles out a representative, 'seated in the sun, with a book in his hand and the wall at his back' as he dreams of attaining the stature of the author he is reading. Hazlitt is himself writing, of course, and, in entertaining nostalgia for a boy's burning ambition to excel at his own profession, he playfully invites the boy to take over: 'Come hither, thou poor little fellow, and let us change places with thee if thou wilt; here take the pen and finish this article'. Dialogically hailing the reader in the same way, he invites us to imagine that Sir Francis Bourgeois' motive for donating his art collection to the school in 1811 was to soften his approach to death 'by being associated with the hopes of childhood' in raising a monument to himself in a charitably founded school amidst '"the innocence and simplicity of poor *Charity Boys*!" Might it not have been so?', he asks the reader (p. 18). A series of youthful surrogates, therefore, both singular and typical, shuttle back and forth across the ages to activate each other in shifting their attention between reading, looking and thinking in a playful attitude that culminates in the contemplation of an art gallery as the illustration of a philosophical theory. Playfulness is the educational purpose of stimulating credulous schoolboys to wonder at 'a world of art' experienced as 'an enchanting deception'. The relevance of Molyneux's question to the passage, however, consists in children looking for the first time not at the *external world* but at *paintings*.

In this respect, the first meaning of 'sort of illustration' as proof rather than spoof of Berkeley's theory comes to the fore. True, Hazlitt powerfully invokes the *fiction* of Macbeth's dagger 'palpable to feeling as to sight' (1823, vol. 10, 19), but the point, again, is the reality of illusion, not the illusion of reality. Likewise, while vividly declaring its irrelevance to Cuyp's scene, the 'down on an unripe nectarine' invites us to screw up our mental eyes to look for something that is not there, for neither ripe nor unripe nectarines grow down (the *OED* definition of 1616 describes a nectarine as a 'variety of common peach, with a thinner and downless skin'). The analogy refers not to the scenery itself, however, but its ethereal effect, and, just as the globe metaphor enlarged Wilson's *Apollo*, so is there a magical enlargement of scale here as 'a province is contained in a foot of canvas' (Hazlitt 1823, vol. 10, 19).

Together with the hardening of shadows and the laying on of fingers, this effect suggests that Hazlitt was thinking of the equivocal wonderland that a young patient called Daniel Dolins reported to the surgeon William Cheselden after a cataract operation performed in 1727 enabled him to see paintings for the first time. What was new was not the operation but Cheselden's report on the patient's thoughts and feelings (1728), which interested Berkeley and Hazlitt because it raised 'questions not about the origins of ideas, but about the sensory sources of sensibility' (Riskin 2002, 34). The case would have been familiar to Hazlitt from Berkeley's quotation of it in his *Theory of Vision* as proof of his negative answer to Molyneux's question. Indeed there is some evidence to suggest that Berkeley, who had social ties with Cheselden and the patient's family, co-authored the report with Cheselden, since it employs vocabulary that is typical of the philosopher but not of the surgeon (Leffler et al. 2021, 102–5, 109–10). The patient expected that 'pictures would feel like the things they represented, and was amaz'd when he found those parts, which by their light and shadow appear'd now round and uneven, felt only flat like the rest; and asked which was the lying sense, feeling, or seeing?' (Cheselden 1728, 449; partially quoted in Berkeley 1733, 59).

Cheselden had reported that his patient experienced the regaining of vision as gradual and disturbing. It took two months for him to realize that portraits represented solid objects (Hirschberg 1985, vol. 2, 298). With only occasional exceptions, Cheselden's findings were accepted by other surgeons performing similar operations for well over a century (pp. 298–308), but today they are rejected as a test of Molyneux's question (Hirschberg 1985, vol. 2, 310; Leffler et al. 2021, 106), for, if cataracts are not removed by the age of two months and certainly by eight years, a condition of amblyopia sets in due to insufficient brain plasticity that prevents eyes from working together, blurs central vision and impairs depth perception (Hirschberg 1985, vol. 2, 310).[3] Cheselden's patient was thirteen (Leffler et al. 2021, 103–4). Nevertheless, Hazlitt's response to Cuyp's painting as 'another universe' was underpinned by scientific evidence considered legitimate in its day. The power of his critique is largely due to its blend of scientific fact and philosophically inspired speculation that embodied the material in the immaterial as a quality he prized in art (Hazlitt 1823, vol. 10, 19).

4 Hazlitt on Poussin

Hazlitt had channelled Berkeley and Cheselden before in his essay 'On a Landscape of Nicolas Poussin' (1821) where he evoked the mythological aura of the blind giant Orion being restored to sight in the celebrated description of *Blind Orion Searching for the Rising Sun* (1658; **Figure 4**).

> ORION, the subject of this landscape, was the classical Nimrod; and is called by Homer, 'a hunter of shadows, himself a shade'. He was the son of

Figure 4 Nicolas Poussin, *Blind Orion Searching for the Rising Sun*, 1658. Oil on canvas, 119.1 × 182.9 cm, Metropolitan Museum of Art, New York, Fletcher Fund, 1924, Accession number 24.451

---

[3] Confirmed by Professor Bill Morgan, co-director of the Lions Eye Institute, Perth, Australia, interviewed 5 November 2020.

Neptune; and having lost an eye in some affray between the Gods and men, was told that if he would go to meet the rising sun, he would recover his sight. He is represented setting out on his journey, with men on his shoulder to guide him, a bow in his hand, and Diana in the clouds greeting him. He stalks along, a giant upon earth, and reels and falters in his gait, as if just awaked out of sleep, or uncertain of his way; – you see his blindness, though his back is turned. Mists rise around him, and veil the sides of the green forests; earth is dank and fresh with dews, the 'grey dawn and the Pleiades before him dance', and in the distance are seen the blue hills and sullen ocean. Nothing was ever more finely conceived or done. It breathes the spirit of the morning; its moisture, its repose, its obscurity, waiting the miracle of light to kindle it into smiles: the whole is, like the principle figure in it, 'a forerunner of the dawn'. The same atmosphere tinges and imbues every object, the same dull light 'shadowy sets off' the face of nature: one feeling of vastness, of strangeness, and of primeval forms pervades the painter's canvas, and we are thrown back upon the first integrity of things.

(Hazlitt 1821, vol. 8, 168–169)

Again we have the intimate glance into internal perception, separated by a dash from the rest '– you see his blindness, though his back is turned' – but on this occasion the tropes of Molyneux, Locke, Berkeley and Cheselden play more loosely about the description because the protagonist is not completely blind but one-eyed due to a battle with the gods. His predicament resembles the intermediary state of the blind man in the gospel of St Mark who at first sees only men like trees walking and must await Christ's second touch to see fully (8: 22–6). The word 'miracle' is used (Hazlitt 1821, 173) and the Bible has already been invoked in 'Nimrod', 'a mighty Hunter before the Lord' (Genesis 10: 9; Paulin 1998, 209).

What does it mean 'to see his blindness, though his back is turned'? We do see one closed eye in Orion's painted profile, but Hazlitt means that we share his view of blindness. Milton embedded a dialectic between externally and internally viewed blindness in his Sonnet 22 to Cyriack, which was written with Molyneux's question and 'the cultural tensions between the claims of idealist philosophy and the claims of the materialists' in mind (Van Den Berg 2009, 19). Hazlitt quotes the poem in full in his essay 'On Milton's Sonnets', written the year after the Poussin essay and next in order in *The Round Table*. Milton revealed that sighted people cannot see that he is blind because his eyes are 'clear / To outward view, of blemish or of spot', and he rejoices that, 'in liberty's defence', blindness has conferred on him the capacity for spiritual and moral foresight denied to others. Hazlitt relished Milton's support of the Cromwellian Revolution. Though blind, Milton penetrates 'the world's vain mask' with 'no better guide' than revolutionary thought (quoted by Hazlitt 1822c, vol. 8, 177).

Christ, too, had manually guided the blind man in St Mark before curing him. It was a two-stage process in which the restoration of physical vision was followed by the gift of spiritual insight (Glenney 2014, 74–5). One thinks of the men on Orion's shoulders guiding him towards enlightening dawn and the way in which, as Tom Paulin has shown, Hazlitt's rhetoric in the essay embeds a tide of collective pro-revolutionary sentiment, including the Napoleonic 'advance of history towards the rising sun of republican forms of government' (Paulin 1998, 213). The advance identifies Orion with the blind, visionary poets Homer and Milton, who 'never ceased to imagine a restored Commonwealth' (p. 217). As quoted at the beginning of this section, Homer called Orion 'a hunter of shadows, himself a shade'. At the end Hazlitt calls Napoleon, who had died that year, 'the hunter of greatness and of glory ... himself a shade!' (1821, p. 174). As well as looking back towards primordial nature (p. 169), the light of restored vision shows the path towards future revolution, for, despite Napoleon's death, his 'deeds ... are re-enacted in the afterlife that is posterity' (p. 210). Associating Hazlitt's Dissenting Unitarian upbringing with the philosopher Jean-Jacques Rousseau, Paulin regards the Poussin essay as 'an elegy for Unitarianism with its republican idealism, faith in progress, and devotion to the primitive Church' (p. 218). Proactive envisioning is therefore spiritual as well as moral, political and classical. Orion, Homer, Milton, Napoleon, Rousseau, the Unitarian Church, Hazlitt, Rousseau and the reader are symbolically identified in a narrative of generative reflexivity as strong as the amalgamation of schoolboys and adults activating each others' futures in 'Dulwich Art Gallery'.

Like Cheselden's case, there is an alternation between appearance and reality as paintings teach us how 'to dream and be awake at the same time' (Hazlitt 1821, vol. 8, 173), but there is also a more complex dialectic of blindness and revelation as one veil of sight begets another in a mise en abyme of proactive visions. Returning to the opening description, we see Orion 'presented', first in history then in the painting. As Hazlitt reconstructs it, the landscape does not, as we might expect, show us the landscape Orion cannot see. Rather, the viewer fuses with Orion in 'seeing' his partial blindness in a landscape masked by clouds before the sun rises to restore his vision. The landscape represents both his semi-blindness and the scene before him by standing for and replicating Orion's occluded retina, while the 'sides' of forests veiled by mists is a choice of words that highlights the fact that objects, including blinded eyes, have different sides to be looked at. Fully embedded now in the 'antique gusto' (p. 179) of Orion's full sensorium, we share his envelopment by the odour of the earth, 'dank and fresh with dew', which Paulin interprets as an admission of the blood shed by revolutionaries (p. 218). The quotation of 'grey dawn and the Pleiades before him dance' from *Paradise Lost* (2005, sec. 8, ll. 374–5) enjoins us to the blind Milton's imagination, for there are no such details in Poussin's sky. True, 'the blue hills and sullen ocean' resemble the horizon, but they too are tokens of pathetic fallacy and inner vision for reasons stated in the opening sentence of 'Why Distant Objects Please': 'Distant objects please, because … not being obtruded too close upon the eye, we clothe them with the indistinct and airy colours of fancy' (Hazlitt 1822b, vol. 8, 255). That essay also demonstrated that retinal images not only depend on tactile journeys for spatialization but also instigate them. 'When I was a boy, I lived within sight of a range of lofty hills, whose blue tops blending with the setting sun had often tempted my longing eyes and wandering feet.' Retinal images of distant objects are anticipative as well as recollective, even if, at journey's end, they collapse into 'huge lumpish heaps of discoloured earth' like bad paintings of unfamiliar places, for the 'fancy colours the prospect of the future as it thinks good' (p. 256).

A breathing metaphor then envelops the reader in an oceanic effect of moist atmosphere that 'tinges and imbues every object' with 'one feeling of vastness'. But envelopment rapidly succeeds to violent action as 'we are thrown back upon the first integrity of things'. The pace has quickened throughout the passage, from stumbling to forerunning to this catapulting of the spectator into the flat 'canvas' that has just been mentioned, where he or she is instantly reconstituted as three-dimensional subject matter, 'original nature, full, solid, large, luxurious, teeming with life and power' (p. 169), which reverses Wilson's reduction of British scenery to flat molehills and cockleshells. It is another exchange of places where we no longer see nature at a distance through Orion's hampered vision but become what it beheld, a reversal which happens again later in the 'looks' of figures in paintings, 'which only the looks of the spectator can express' (p. 173). Certainly, this strange impact dazes us. We are thrown back in time, but in which physical direction: backwards or forwards? And from what point of view? Yet the phrase remains viscerally apt to the mental impact of good painting, for it lends active form to a negative event: the suspension of disbelief that happens when we forget pigment and give ourselves over to an imaginary world. Sensation embodies an ineffable mental event.

Being thrown against 'the first integrity of things' resounds throughout the essay in other reversals of blindness and revelation. Regaining vision, Orion is suddenly granted a lifting power and overview on par with the artist and God as all three enact a perceptual enlargement of scale we are by now familiar with from descriptions of Wilson and Cuyp. 'Like his own Orion, [the artist] overlooks the surrounding scene, appears to "take up the isles as a very little thing, and to lay the earth in a balance"' (p. 169). Hazlitt elides two misquotations from Isiah about God's power over the earth (40: 16 and 12), though the power is also Napoleon's again (Paulin 1998, 224).

Muscular metaphors continue to proliferate in an increasingly generic account of the creative process, which now includes literature. Poussin 'was among painters (more than any one else) what Milton was among poets' (Hazlitt 1821, vol. 8, 169). In an argument familiar from his need to retain naturalism in imaginative history painting and epic literature, Hazlitt has artists define the shape of these apparently fixed containers by crushing nature into them, but they still leak back into the natural realm because Poussin's 'art is a second nature, not a different one' (p. 170; see Bromwich 1983, 215 and ff.).

Hazlitt closes with a meditation on two ways in which knowledge of art spreads. First, works are 'scattered' physically 'like stray gifts through the world' (p. 174). As a quotation from Wordsworth, this sounds Romantically random, but Poussin's *Orion* is just one of many paintings released from aristocratic collections to 'enrich the public eye' at annual British Institution exhibitions (p. 173). The essay concludes by reminding the readership that many of these paintings came from Wellington's sacking of the great public gallery of the Louvre to teach the French what he considered was a moral lesson about stealing from other nations. The Louvre, which included much spoil from Napoleon's conquest of countries he regarded as despotic, had been reorganized to decontextualize religious and aristocratic art and recontextualize it in the future public sphere. This is partly what Hazlitt meant by reversing the temporal coordinates of nature in Poussin's *Orion* from the past to the future so as to 'transport us to distant places, and join the regions of imagination (a new conquest) to those of reality', by he (meaning Poussin, Napoleon and the others) 'who teaches us not only what nature is, but what she has been, and is capable of being' (p. 169).

By analogy with political conquest, conquering regions of the imagination is the second way paintings spread. To turn paintings into words is to mentalize and mobilize them. The process again resembles the Berkeleyan embodying of the material in the immaterial in Hazlitt's description of Cuyp. Collections, as well as paintings, inhabit mental space. Containing 'chosen images', they are 'a stream of pleasant thoughts passing through the mind' (p. 173). As such they are a 'luxury', a refuge from reality, but they also 'multiply with the desire of the mind to see more and more of them: as if there were a living power in the breath of Fame, and in the very names of the great heirs of glory "there were propagation too"' (pp. 173–4). In other words: they civilize.

Nothing in the essay particularly suggests that Hazlitt is thinking of the American Revolution as well as the French one. Yet the 'conquest' of primal nature 'in distant places' suggests geographical as well as temporal distance.

Certainly, the forward-looking tide of political, religious and poetic associations coincides with the pro-American, Non-Conformist leanings of his father, whom he had accompanied to America as a child when he preached as one of the first Unitarian ministers there. But if 'aboriginal scene' (p. 169) includes New World wilderness as well as classical Arcadia, a schism opens up between the soft diplomacy of European imaginative vision and American politics and religion. In 1829 Hazlitt declared: 'I am by education and conviction inclined to republicanism and puritanism. In America they have both.' But he then feels compelled to ask: 'Can they throughout the United States, from Boston to Baltimore, produce a single head like one of Titian's Venetian nobles, nurtured in all the pride of aristocracy and all the blindness of popery' (1930–4, vol. 20, 283)? Culturally, it is Americans, not papists, who are blind. The fixed containers of the European imagination do not incorporate foreign culture, for none is to be had.

Even when Hazlitt considers travel writing and scientific illustration, 'the effect of novelty in exciting the attention, may account, perhaps, for the extraordinary discoveries and lies told by travellers, who, opening their eyes for the first time in foreign parts, are startled at every object they see' (1930–4, vol. 4, 75). Like seeing for the first time in Cheselden's case, Hazlitt is interested in the novelty of equivocal effects, not in what foreign places are really like. The rupture between the perceiving soul and material world that Ernst Cassirer posited as the core determinant of Enlightenment debates between empiricism and idealism finds its counterpart in Hazlitt's multiplication of and oscillation between ontological realms, be they internal and external, real and imaginary, natural and mythological, the classical past and the revolutionary future, or perhaps even Europe and its former colonies. Meanwhile his preoccupation with the growth of something vast from something small in the spectator's sensory perception of painting, of something solid from something flat, and something future-bound from primordial wilderness anticipates Ruskin's reception of his writings and American responses to Molyneux's question.

5 Ruskin's 'Innocence of the Eye'

The basic tenet of Ruskin's early writing in defence of J. M. W. Turner's painting – that artists should go to nature 'rejecting nothing, selecting nothing, and scorning nothing' (Ruskin 1843, vol. 3, 624) – clearly draws on Hazlitt's attack on Reynold's Neoclassical theory of general forms; but as Hazlitt's pious successor, who was far more deeply versed in theological sciences that sought to reconcile the teachings of the Bible with natural evidence of the Creation,

Ruskin was insistent on searching for religious absolutes in the totality of natural phenomena.

Thus, Hazlitt's meditation on Cuyp's *Herdsmen with Cows* quoted in *Modern Painters I* (Ruskin 1843) brought a thundering denunciation from Ruskin, which centred on that wayward analogy with the nectarine: 'I ought to have apologized before now for not having studied sufficiently in Covent Garden to be provided with terms of correct and classical criticism . . . Now I dare say that the sky of this first-rate Cuyp is very like an unripe nectarine: all that I have to say is, that it is exceedingly unlike a sky' (vol. 3, 350). The jibe snobbishly demotes Hazlitt to a Cockney barrow boy, but it also points to the urban tenor of his nectarine analogy. Ruskin continues with an extended analysis of the graduated colours of actual skies, concluding that 'there is no such thing . . . .. as a serene sunset sky, with its purple and rose in *belts* about the sun' (pp. 350–1; his emphasis). The problem was Cuyp's flatness.

Given this clash, it is curious to discover that, in *The Elements of Drawing*, Ruskin concurred entirely with Hazlitt's understanding of Locke's theory of the flat retinal image, but drew opposite conclusions from it:

> The perception of solid Form is entirely a matter of experience. We *see* nothing but flat colours; and it is only by a series of experiments that we find out that a stain of black or grey indicates the dark side of a solid substance . . . The whole technical power of painting depends on our recovery of what may be called the *innocence of the eye*; that is to say, of a sort of childish perception of these flat stains of colour merely as such, without consciousness of what they signify, – as a blind man would see them if suddenly gifted with sight. (1857, vol. 15, 27 n.; his emphases)

The artist must free himself of habit by stripping away from retinal images exactly those synaesthetic associations that were essential to Hazlitt to find either imitative or imaginative conviction in illusions of distance and solidity. Utterly discounting the value of habitual memories, the footnote continues:

> We go through such processes of experiment unconsciously in childhood; and having once come to conclusions touching the signification of certain colours, we always suppose that we *see* what we only know, and have hardly any consciousness of the real aspect of the signs we have learned to interpret.
>
> Now, a highly accomplished artist has always reduced himself as nearly as possible to this condition of infantine sight. (p. 28 n.; his emphasis)

The eye is the ledger on which God writes 'signs'. According to the Evangelical typology in which Ruskin was trained, nature is a Second Bible whose meaning discharges itself in sacred language or symbols. Restoring the innocence of the eye by ousting the pictorial conventions of aesthetic treatises and style manuals allowed theories of perception to influence art making and constituted a powerful bequest to American art and criticism (Georgi 2013, 83).

Ruskin strove to find a religious alternative to Locke's associationist theory of vision to overcome the physiological limitations of the retina and explain artists' acquisition of accurate knowledge of nature. According to Locke, our conception of an object's tertiary qualities (such as the inferred power of the sun upon wax) can only be arrived at through secondary qualities (our perception that the wax is melting), which in turn depend upon primary qualities (the capacity of wax to melt) (1975, 137–43). Using the words 'power', 'force' and eventually 'primo mobile', meaning 'first cause', Ruskin inverted the hierarchy of Locke's three qualities by making tertiary qualities the cause of all the rest (1903–12, vol. 19, 356–7). Famously dismissive of Kant and German transcendental philosophy (vol. 4, 424–6), he reverted to the authority of Plato's *Timaeus* for an extromissionist theory of perception founded on innate ideas. Light, according to Plato, is emitted both from the soul and from God's objects, 'the fact being that the force must be there, and the eyes there; and 'light' means the effect of the one on the other; – and perhaps, also – (Plato saw farther into that mystery than any one has since, that I know of), – on something a little way within the eyes' (1903–12, vol. 18, 343–44). This constituted a feedback loop, whereby the soul is attracted to organic motifs by dint of 'the natural tendency impressed on us by our Creator to love the forms into which the earth He gave us to tread, and out of which He formed our bodies, knit itself as it was separated from the deep' (1903–12, vol. 9, 271). But it is characteristic of Ruskin to express Platonic ideas in language that echoes Locke: 'I deny not, that there are natural tendencies imprinted on the Minds of Men; and that, from the very first instances of Sense and Perception, there are some things . . . they incline to, and others that they fly', but 'this makes nothing for innate Characters on the Mind' (Locke 1975, 67).

Their different enactments of sensory perception help to explain Hazlitt's and Ruskin's opposite assessments of Turner. In contrast to Poussin's achievement of 'the first integrity of things', Hazlitt complained that Turner 'delights to go back to the first chaos of the world' and that his landscapes "were *pictures of nothing, and very like*"' (Hazlitt 1930–4, vol. 4, 76 n; his emphasis). To understand why Poussin produced 'integrity' and Turner 'chaos', we recall that Hazlitt measured a painting's success by its provision of 'salient points for the eye to rest upon or start from' in its journey from one feature to another (vol. 8, 38). This was anathema to Ruskin because fear of idolatry led him to condemn 'solidity of projection' as 'the vilest mechanism that art can be insulted by giving a name to' (1843, vol. 3, 164). By contrast, Turner's 'retirement of solid surface' prevents the spectator's eye from grasping it through touch. In Ruskin's understanding, Turner had dismantled the stage scenery of classical structure and replaced it with the means for inducing a mystical apprehension of distance that far surpassed Claudian depth construction. Ruskin observed that 'if ever an edge is expressed' in Turner's *Mercury and Argus* (1836)

> it is only felt for an instant, and then lost again; so that the eye cannot stop at it and prepare for a long jump to another like it, but is guided over it, and round it into the hollow beyond; and thus the whole receding mass of ground, going back for more than a quarter of a mile, is made completely *one* ... giving ... to the foreground of this universal master precisely the same qualities which we have before seen in the hills, as Claude gave to his foreground ... infinite unity in the one case, finite division in the other.
>
> (Ruskin 1843, vol. 3, 485–6; his emphasis)

Ruskin needed this Platonic supplement to abolish the human agency of Lockean associations in visual perception and renounce the idolatry of touch, a renunciation memorably enacted in *Praeterita,* his late autobiography, when recalling his sketch of an aspen tree at Fontainebleau whose 'beautiful lines insisted on being traced', becoming 'more and more beautiful ... as each rose out of the rest, and took its place in the air' (1885–9, vol. 35, 313). 'Sight', for Ruskin, was 'an absolutely spiritual phenomenon; accurately, and only, to be so defined' (1903–12, vol. 22, 194). Yet he remained an avowed Lockean who believed that 'whatever impressions are made on the outward parts [of the body], if they are not taken notice of within; there is no perception' (1843, vol. 3, 141). Thomas Carlyle's 'spiritual optics' owes a similar, paradoxical debt to both empirical and idealist premises (Budge 2008, 18).

6 History: Molyneux's Question in America

Supersensuous swooping of an eye freed from touch was something that Thomas Cole, an American history painter from England, could not abide when he caught up with Turner's latest works in London in 1829, fourteen years before the publication of *Modern Painters I*: 'They are splendid combinations of colour when it is considered separately from the subject, but they are destitute of all appearance of solidity' (Cole quoted in Barringer and Kornhauser 2018, 166). Moreover, in writing to Cole in Europe about a view from his mansion Cole had painted in the United States (*View of Monte Video, the Seat of Daniel Wadsworth, Esq.,* 1828), Daniel Wadsworth invoked a collapse of spatiality akin to Hazlitt's shrunken mountain and pasteboard globe: 'To us ... Monte Video remains as beautiful as ever ... but after the splendid Mountains [and] Palaces you have lived amongst it will appear but a miniature – & a rude one' (quoted in Barringer 1994, 2). Scale is not the issue here: American history afforded insufficient cultural memory to spatialize the view.

The negative answer to Molyneux's question in Europe was compelled by the cardinal tenet of empiricism: nothing is in the mind that was not first in the senses. In broad terms, empiricism was the guiding philosophy of the colonial project, for there was no better doctrine for grasping the reality of distant territories in order to expropriate, control and exploit Native peoples and their lands. Though cartographic flattenings of three-dimensional terrains depended on the strenuous bodily activity of explorers finding visible and tangible landmarks to fix mathematical coordinates upon that then required several processes of abstraction and inscription, maps taught imperialists how to make distant places familiar so as to reverse the balance of power between masters and mastered (Tobin 1999, 215; Jones 2005).

But if scientific instruments replaced the hands of Molyneux's blind man to pre-empt recognition of distant places, painters of 'New Worlds' (new, at least, to those who colonized them) keenly felt the lack of cultural history that made European landscapes tangibly familiar and culturally intelligible. Thus, when Molyneux's question crossed the Atlantic, negative answers became problematic, for how is the colonial painter to acquire necessary non-visual associations when, as Thomas Cole remarked in a journal entry for 1835, 'all nature here is new to Art' (1980, 131). Thus, in his 'Essay on American Scenery' (1836), Cole addressed 'what has been considered a grand defect in American scenery – the want of associations, such as arise amid the scenes of the old world' (p. 270). Hazlitt certainly shared this view – 'no ghost, we will venture to say, was ever seen in North America' (1930–4, vol. 16, 319) – and *pace* 'the *innocence of the eye*', it was still more Ruskin's view. All the life went out of a tender Alpine scene when he transported it in the eye of his imagination to 'some aboriginal forest' in the Americas. 'The flowers in an instant lost their light, the river its music; the hills became oppressively desolate; a heaviness in the boughs of the darkened forest showed how much of their former power had been dependent upon a life which was not theirs … the deep colours of human endurance, valour and virtue' (Hazlitt 1902–13, vol. 8, 223–34). Such views would not remain unchallenged in America (see **Section 7**).

If the inferior art of landscape painting was to elevate colonial taste as it ought, it must emulate the prestige of history painting by employing scenery transformed by heroic action, as Claude, Poussin and other European painters had done. According to Locke, retinal images are unintelligible without prior tactile experience of the objects they register, hence the difficulty for artists making, or writers appraising, paintings of untouched Nature. Yet if Locke's theory of perception was partly responsible for this evacuation of life-enhancing associations, his other writings provided a rationale for two great historical themes that were amply available to American memory: 'the great struggle for freedom', as Thomas Cole called the War of Independence (1836, 270), and the clearing of wilderness.

As a vindication of the Whig resistance to divine-right monarchy in the wake of the Glorious Revolution, Locke's *Two Treatises on Government* (1689) asserted the free and equal status of all individuals against the hierarchical authority and privilege of divine-right monarchy. This accorded with the new importance of subjective experience that empirical theories of perception granted to autonomous individuals in their social relations. America was on empirical grounds 'a state of nature' (Locke 1689, 30), a testing ground for the integration of Locke's political and perceptual theories. In the chapter on the labour theory of property in the *Second Treatise*, Locke justified property through the exertion of physical labour on natural resources. 'Whatsoever . . . he removes out of the state that nature hath provided, and left it in, he hath mixed his labour with, and joined to it something that is his own, and thereby makes it his property' (p. 28). This particularly applied to agriculture and enclosure. 'He by his labour does, as it were, enclose it from the common' (p. 30), a process exemplified in the 'homestead principle' of independent ownership taken up by Thomas Jefferson (Marx 2000, 73–144), which in no way resembled the aristocratic hierarchy Locke imposed in his town plans for Carolina (Purdy 2015, 75–9). Making property a criterion of citizenship served the interests of an empire based on freedom but also justified the dispossession of Native Americans wrongly supposed ignorant and incapable of agriculture (Arneil 1996). Locke's preoccupation with land efficiency in the *Second Treatise* made Indigenous cultural priorities unthinkable: 'for I ask, whether in the wild wood and uncultivated waste of America, left to nature, without any improvement, tillage, or husbandry, a thousand acres yield the needy and wretched inhabitants as many conveniencies [sic] of life as ten acres equally fertile land do in Devonshire, where they are well cultivated' (1689, 33). Physical effort in clearing land coincided with the tactile element in visual perception and implicitly conferred on settlers the citizenship denied to First Americans.

View of a Manor House on the Harlem River, New York (1793) by the newly arrived Englishman William Groombridge is a good example of the tactile sight lines used in many American landscape paintings to reinforce the connections between Lockean perception, property enclosure and American national history (**Figure 5**). Looking north or north-east from the tip of upper Manhattan Island,

Figure 5 William Groombridge, *View of Manor House on the Harlem River, New York*, 1793, oil on canvas, 101 × 124.5 cm, Terra Foundation for American Art, Daniel J. Terra Collection, 1992.37

we see pasture lands receding to the manor house on the left while, at the centre, a cluster of houses and fields taper along the Harlem River flowing behind them to the right. On the far side of the river, now the Bronx, verdant hillsides recede in the distance. Land improvement cannot be extricated from its defining opposite, wilderness. The abrupt hillock disfigured by erosion and cropped on the right is a *repoussoir* that interpolates us looking from wilderness onto civilization. From rough uncultivated terrain, the prospect of ordered settlement unfolds on either side of a road that curves through the space of fenced arable land towards trim houses and outhouses before wilderness resumes towards the horizon, pricked by a distant church steeple that hails further settlement. Oblique violence attends the spectator's entrance into the picture space, for the artist reported that, in making the painting, 'I will dash a watermelon to pieces, and make a foreground of it' (Groombridge quoted in Dunlap 1969, vol. 2, 47–8). Perhaps he is emulating Gilpin's cheerful vandalism in recommending 'the mallet rather than the chisel' to 'beat down' and 'deface' nature 'and throw the mutilated members round in heaps' (1794, 7). Forcing nature into violent compliance with picturesque conventions had euphemized the

British enclosure movement's expropriation of the Commons. Here, though, it chimes in with relics of fierce battles in the American Revolution that had taken place only fourteen years earlier. One of the houses towards the centre of the village is partly ruined, perhaps by cannon fire, while the double walls 'of uncertain height and function' surmounted by triangular pediments at bottom right are obsolete fortifications that further demarcate wilderness from civilization (Monks 2018, 18). If America had not won the War of Independence, this peaceful community would not be thriving as it promises still to do.

The emotional prospect of a glorious future seems to enshrine a political ideology sharply distinct from the social organization of the 'old country'. Crucial here is the bent form of the farmworker who trudges from left to right with his lower half occluded by the rough terrain of the rising foreground, another margin between settlement and wilderness. In one sense he is just 'staffage' animating the landscape, but his movement is vital to the overall composition. Like a perpetual motion machine, his gait constantly winds our eye past the cattle and fields towards the hillock on the right, where it is released like a pinball diagonally upwards into the radiant sky where the common sociality and expansive freedom of the scene is joyously celebrated. Were this Britain, it would be easy to imagine him a victim of the enclosure movement, turned from a free existence on the Commons into a rural wage slave. But this is America, where the war was supposed to have consigned feudal and capitalist exploitation to the past. His colourful clothing suggests a modicum of prosperity consistent with the social ideology of independent freeholders or yeoman farmers set forth in Thomas Jefferson's Ordinance Act of 1784 (Cosgrove 2008, 94–96). Within this vision Groombridge's trudging farmer, the fences that arc behind him and the spreading radiance of the sky are tactile sight lines that dramatize a history of heroic action, for 'the virtues of the new nation are to be found ... in the hearts of those who labour in the earth' (Jefferson quoted in Cosgrove 1984, 176). Sight in the service of proprietorial touch fostered heroic alterations of landscape that, like Hazlitt's *Orion*, summoned visions of the future as much as the past. Thus, Cole again: 'in looking over the yet uncultivated scene, the mind's eye may see far into futurity. Where the wolf roams, the plough shall glisten' (Cole 1836, 270). We need not wonder how even a newcomer such as Groombridge absorbed these ultimately Lockean values, for 'accounts of natural law and progress were the staples of political speeches, sermons, popular writing, and agricultural journals. One did not have to be a reader of jurisprudence or philosophy' (Purdy 2015, 77–8).

Angela Miller has argued that Cole's American paintings are deeply indebted to 'a form of sensationalism, traceable to John Locke, in which the mind and imagination were seen as imprinted with the sensory data of particular environments'. Shared in common through accumulated sensory experience in which innate ideas played no part, 'national character', as the 'transcript' of scenery, became a symbol of American exceptionalism (Miller 1993, 9). In the influential lecture *The Significance of the Frontier in American History* that Frederick Jackson Turner delivered and published in 1893, consciousness of a Lockean sense of character formation through the imprint of localities on the immigrant imagination became a fully wrought dialectic between successive phases of the advancing frontier. The metaphors of expansion we encountered in Hazlitt now correlate with the 'expansive power' of the 'universal disposition of Americans to emigrate to the western wilderness, in order to enlarge their dominion over inanimate nature' (Frederick Turner 2008, 7, 6). Each successive frontier was supposed to have added a new layer to the palimpsest of American character (p. 8). Though bereft of history, America recapitulates 'the course of universal history' read backwards in space and time from the Western frontier to its Eastern origins (p. 10). This emulates the consecutive stages of history, from hunting and gathering through pastoralism and agriculture to commerce laid down by Scottish enlightenment philosophers, and restates Thomas Jefferson's 'survey, in time, of the progress of man from the infancy of man to the present day' encountered by the philosophical traveller 'from the savages of the Rocky Mountains eastwardly towards our sea coast' (quoted in Dixon 1986, 80). Turner's mix of informality, violence, initiative and democracy epitomized by the unruly presidency of President Andrew Jackson was a recognisable version of the Lockean liberal ethos of material values, economic self-interest and individualism. According to this view, American character is the outcome of dialectical struggle between the resistance of nature and the momentum of colonization.

But if scenery lacked the richness of other nations' histories, the landscape of personal history was always available to home-born American artists. Rebecca Bedell has recounted how Cole, Asher Brown Durand and others painted a sentimental genre of landscape that appeased culturally unremarkable scenery with memories of their own or their patrons' childhood, often including a path that walked the spectator down memory lane into a Claudian framework of personalized reminiscence. In Durand's *Study from Nature: Stratton Notch, Vermont* (1853), painted for the lawyer Mark Skinner, a fallen tree blocks the pathway. 'To cross it is to move from the concrete specificity and tactility of the physical, phenomenal world into the mistier realm of memory' (Bedell 2018, 93). But to generate sentimental reminiscence for the spectators of any landscape, not just the one they grew up in, Durand crafted a technique of looking in his influential 'Letters on Landscape Painting' that enlisted the support of Archibald Alison. Letter IV charts the daydreams of a 'rich merchant and capitalist' who grew up in the country but made his fortune in the city. Relaxing in an armchair with a couple of landscape paintings to ruminate upon after a day of drudgery in the city, he makes 'no greater effort than to look into the picture rather than on it' (Durand 1854, 294). This is the crucial stage in Lockean perception when memory inflates two-dimensional impressions into three-dimensional experiences, but here the owner soon abandons the stimulus of the painting to float along trains of association of which Alison had written that 'the object itself, appears only to serve as a hint, to awaken the imagination, and to lead it through every analogous idea that has place in the memory' (p. 42). Alison also defined the potency of specifically autobiographical trains of sentiment: 'The view of the house where one was born, of the school where one was educated, and where the gay years of infancy were passed ... lead ... to so long a train of feelings and recollections, that there is hardly any scene which one ever beholds with so much rapture' (p. 15). Accordingly, Durand's owner, with a happier outcome than Hazlitt's use of Alison on Wilson (see **Section 2**), experiences a sequence of blissful memories as, with some volition, he 'shifts the scene' from the representation before him to discontinuous images from his idyllic rural childhood, from which 'ambition whispered that the village grounds were too narrow for him, – and with the last rays of the setting sun, the picture fades away' (p. 295). Urban ambitions are endorsed, but commercial greed, including the sales pitch of Durand's own Letter, is tempered by the piety of Wordsworthian intimations of immortality. In this way the history of national progress through mass migrations to the city is recapitulated within the individual psyche without sacrificing pastoral values.

Ruskin's repudiation of sensuous greed was one of his chief bequests to American art and criticism (Georgi 2013), but Americans also adopted an earlier advocate of aesthetic renunciation. In the following well-known passage from his 'Essays on the Pleasures of the Imagination' in *The Spectator* – assumed reading for the upwardly mobile classes in America (Bellion 2011, 19 and n.21) – Joseph Addison appeared to elevate a new class of middle-class connoisseurs by granting them aesthetic ownership of what the landed gentry owned in plenty and the vulgar not at all:

> A man of polite imagination is let into a great many pleasures, that the vulgar are not capable of receiving. He ... often feels a greater satisfaction in the prospect of fields and meadows, than another does in the possession. It gives him, indeed, a kind of property in everything he sees, and makes the most rude, uncultivated parts of nature administer to his pleasures: so that he looks upon the world, as it were, in another light, and discovers in it a multitude of charms, that conceal themselves from the generality of mankind.
>
> (Addison 1710, 538)

Addison was the first to base a theory of aesthetics on Locke's prioritisation of the senses, particularly vision. Here, like Alison, he is exercising a faculty of active imagination on passively received ideas, writing in the same essay: 'We cannot indeed have a single Image in the Fancy that did not make its first Entrance through the Sight' (p. 537). He was also the first to join Locke's theories of perception and property to form the bourgeois aesthetic subject, for, in the passage already quoted, sight is conceived of as a vicarious form of tactile possession (Winckles 2010). The apparent snobbery of elevating the middle classes by associating the values of the gentry with those of the vulgar reflects the conservative politics of English tourism, which, indifferent to the unequal distribution of land, preserved the status quo by encouraging 'people to enjoy another property without wanting to appropriate it as their own' (Fabricant 1987, 267). But to look 'upon the world ... in another light' also reflects an older tradition of theological revelation that frees the virtuous from the bonds of earthly materialism. Like Gilpin's theory of the picturesque and Ruskin's 'innocence of the eye', Addison's 'innocent pleasures' (3: 359) had religious import. In Addison's case they were inspired by the visionary experience of Andrenio in Baltasar Gracián's Spanish novel *El Criticón*, who, like Molyneux's blind man, emerged from his cave as 'the first man' to perceive 'the grand Theatre of Heaven and Earth ... concealed from those who may freely walk and look around in it from birth to death' (Szécsényi 2017, 595–6). The disinterestedness of imaginative perception eradicates the moral blindness of philistine prestige in ownership.

Ralph Waldo Emerson's Latitudinarian background sensitized him to this visionary component in Addison when he reworked it for American conditions in his influential essay on 'Nature' (1836).

> The charming landscape which I saw this morning, is indubitably made up of some twenty or thirty farms. Miller owns this field, Locke that, and Manning the woodland beyond. But none of them owns the landscape. There is a property in the horizon which no man has but he whose eye can integrate all the parts, that is, the poet. This is the best part of these men's farms, yet to this their warranty-deeds give no title. (Emerson 1836, vol. 1, 9)

There is a world of difference between Addison's 'kind of property' and Emerson's 'property in the horizon', however. The first blurs and the second sharpens the distinction between two meanings of property as 'landed estate' and 'attribute and quality' (OED), as in 'charming landscape'. Unable to be owned, the horizon lifts eyes in religious communion freed from acquisitive competition. The major difference in the sociology of the two passages is that, while both eschew ownership values, Emerson inducts owners, not aesthetes, into his visionary club of taste. Ownership of property is very much the prerequisite of Emerson's transcendental 'property in the horizon', since the philistines he targets are freeholders caught in the communal disunity of the Lockean homestead principle rather than the feudal relations of Addison's landed gentry. It is no coincidence that Emerson names one of his benighted landowners 'Locke'.

As Addison's concept of vicarious possession encompassed both 'the rude uncultivated parts of nature' and 'fields and meadows', so Emerson includes both 'farms' and 'woodland beyond' in his chosen view. Though no single painting presents itself as the source of this poetically integrated scene, Emerson's compositional mode is also pictorial, for this is the archetypical expression of 'the pastoral ideal of America', defined by Leo Marx as 'middle ground somewhere "between," yet in transcendent relation to, the opposing forces of civilization and nature' (Marx 2000, pp. 93, 23). Karl Kusserow argues that the picturesque style of painting lasted longer in America than in Britain not because of cultural lag but because Americans felt threatened by vaster tracts of uncleared wilderness (2018a, 90–1). Emerson writes in 'The Young American' of 'the nervous rocky West intruding a new and continental element into the national mind ... How much better when the whole land is a garden' (1844b, vol. 1, 229). In an early nineteenth-century work, John Trumbull demonstrated how acutely picturesque conventions were needed to contain the sublime excesses of nature (**Figure 6**). His zigzag sight lines are drawn tauter than in any Claude or Wilson to incorporate the edges of Niagara Falls into an impression of cultivated parkland extending to the Canadian side of the river. Only one sheet of falling water and a spume of mist rising from the horizontally angled cataract attests to the thundering might of what has been supressed to accommodate the polite sensibility of the artist and strollers in the foreground (Wolf 1982, 209).

Later in the century the aesthetic sensibility of vicarious possession is inverted. Aesthetic pleasure in land owned by others is replaced by the imaginative prospect of owning others' land. To modern eyes few paintings express the hypocrisy of the nation's 'manifest destiny to overspread the continent allotted by Providence for the free development of our yearly multiplying millions', as John L. O'Sullivan wrote in 1845 (quoted in Brownlee 2008, 26), more painfully than Albert Bierstadt's elegiac portrait of the Yakima people in *Mount Adams, Washington* (1875). Visual traction is supplied by the wishful thinking that Yakima horsemen are voluntarily abandoning their land, which in fact they had cultivated. The central horseman slowly leads the rest of the tribe into the metaphorical darkness of 'manifestly confected' mist on the right (Kusserow 2018b, 128). In other paintings, clouds vicariously sweep serene plains between

Figure 6 John Trumbull, American, 1756–1843, *Niagara Falls from an Upper
Bank on the British Side*, 1807. Oil on canvas, 61.9 × 92.9 cm, Wadsworth
Atheneum Museum of Art, Hartford, CT, Bequest of Daniel Wadsworth, 1848.4

majestic mountains suggesting lust for social and economic as well as imaginative possession (Miller 2001, 48), while views of countries outside America's
national borders become 'increasingly proprietorial' in their expression of
imperial ambitions (Manthorne 1989, 4). George Catlin split actual and aesthetic possession apart completely in his justification for seeking to picture the
habitus of native American peoples doomed to extinction by Manifest Destiny:
'I have flown to their rescue – not of their lives or of their race (for they are
"*doomed*" and must perish), but . . . of their looks and their modes, at which the
acquisitive world may hurl their poison and every besom of destruction, . . . yet
phoenix-like, they may rise from the "stain on a painter's palette," and live again
upon canvas' (Catlin 1995, vol. 1, 16; his emphasis). 'Stain', in this context, is
a dizzying euphemism that disavows blood and guilt as paint.

Finally, landscape painting was historically animated by the narrative thrust
of American fiction. Published in 1826, Fenimore Cooper's *The Last of the
Mohicans* is one of a spate of novels in which genocidal horrors are distanced by
the romantic aura of history, for the novel is set in the relatively deep American
past of the French-Indian war sixty years earlier. In Thomas Cole's *Landscape
with Figures: A Scene from 'The Last of the Mohicans'*, painted in the same year
as the novel from which it takes its title and historical resonances, the tactile
inferences of Molyneux's question are writ large in vectors that seek to establish

Figure 7 Thomas Cole, *Landscape with Figures: A Scene from 'The Last of the Mohicans'*, 1826, oil on panel, 66.4 × 109.4 cm, Terra Foundation for American Art, Daniel J. Terra Collection, 1993.2

dramatic conviction for incidents compounded from the denouement of the novel (**Figure 7**). A euphemistic allegory of Indigenous extinction unfolds across the foreground as our eyes follow the gaze and gestures of the characters from left to right across the stage-set of a rocky plateau towards an abysmal chasm where the native villain meets his death (Parry 2001).

Thereafter there is Baroque effect in the broad, zigzag trajectory that draws the eye backwards and upwards from the foreground into the distance as Cooper's narrative about the past succeeds to Cole's ambivalent specula-tions about the future. Tonally contrasted bands of wilderness approach a brightly lit settlement from which smoke rises, then the sight line rises into the sky and divides around either side of the central mountains that form the horizon. The distant, starkly illuminated settlement overflowing neigh-bouring valleys promises a bright future. But ominous storms descend to the left of the distant mountains to connect with a vector of smoke drifting in their direction from a burning section of the township on the right, suggesting either land clearance or urban conflagration. These forking pathways for the eye on either side of the mountains – bright to the right, dark to the left – set future intimations of manifest destiny against the prospect of divine retribu-tion for despoliation of the land, a pessimistic alternative strengthened by ecological damage from the tanning industry implied by the falling storm and rising fire in the closely related *Catskill Mountain House: The Four*

Elements (1843; Raab 2018, 152–3). Cole is responding to a profound tension in Locke's American heritage. While Locke's homestead principle in the *Second Treatise* promoted personal freedom and profit through the acquisition of property, it also set strict limits: 'what portion [of land] a man carved to himself was easily seen: and it was useless, as well as dishonest, to carve himself too much, or take more than he needed' (Locke 2005, 39). This was a profound tension in Puritan theology (Bilbro 2015, 1–24). What remains constant in both optimistic and pessimistic depictions of environmental change in Hudson River School paintings by Cole and others is the dynamic realization of landscape depth by deep tactile intrusion.

7 Geology

A potent alternative to colonial history as a source of landscape narrative was the scientific study of landforms whose prestige rested on the divine authorship of creation, the exceptionalism of American scenery, and the rise of middle-class interest in tourism and geology. In a letter of 1777, Edmund Burke observed that, in the age of exploration, 'we need no longer go to History to trace it in all its stages and periods ... Now the Great map of mankind is unrolled at once; and there is no state or Gradation of barbarism, and no mode of refinement which we have not at the same instant under our View' (quoted in Quilley 2004, 3). The Prussian polymath Alexander Von Humboldt enlarged upon this shift from history to geography for the new sciences of botany, zoology, meteorology and geology – the most popular because most useful science for American settlers – by substituting the equator as the horizontal line uniting the northern and southern hemispheres for the arbitrary vertical line drawn down the Atlantic Ocean to divide the 'Old World' from the 'New'. His conception of the universal connectedness of nature's balancing forces created a global perspective that diffused the privilege that Europeans had bestowed on the Mediterranean scenery of Claude and Poussin. But rather than dispelling the importance of history, geologically informed artists replaced human history with the grander and greater history of the Creation.

Up to 1860 the history of American landscape painting coincided with a period of catastrophic clearing of forests that had covered almost half the country, with incalculable cost to Indigenous populations and ecological balance (Williams 2010). Years later, Frederick Jackson Turner told the origin story of how 'civilization in America has followed the arteries made by geology' as Indian villages 'suggested by nature' grew into settlers' trading posts and cities. 'It is like the steady growth of a complex nervous system for the originally simple, inert continent' (2008, pp. 13–14). By effacing Indigenous agency and eliding genocide, this geological naturalization of human history was aggressively nationalist.

It was not until 1894 that the picturesque and geological appreciations of landscape parted company, when in *The Mountains of California* the geologist John Muir implicitly condemned artists who approached the mountains of the High Sierra merely as 'separable . . . artistic bits capable of being made into warm, sympathetic, lovable pictures with appreciable humanity in them' (Muir 1894, n.p., ch. 4), but by 1845 Cole was already deforming familiar picturesque conventions in *River in the Catskills* to envision the ugly, anti-pastoral destructiveness of railways (Wallach 2002). The afterlife of Molyneux's question in geologically inspired paintings is implicit in a review of Humboldt's books by George Perkins Marsh, who likened the powers of observation required for the study of nature to 'the gift of a new, or rather the recovery of a lost faculty' (1860, 53). This implies empirical learning rather than idealist intuition, yet the tactile associations embedded in Cole's often highly distorted landscapes suggest that divinely contoured geology could replace linear fencing and agriculture to carve out sensorial impressions of depth in landscape paintings. In the same essay Marsh countered Ruskin's attack on the absence of human associations in American landscape with a bitterly sarcastic summary of his views: 'Wanting ancient memories, American landscape can have no present beauty, and that which God created cannot acquire picturesque significance, or rightfully claim to excite human sympathies, till man has consecrated it by his doubtful virtues, his follies, or his crimes' (p. 47). For America's geologically inspired painters, it is God's, not mankind's, manipulation of the landscape that paintings should express. Hence the curious inversion of tactile metaphors in Cole's complaint about the 'improvements of cultivation' at the expense of 'the sublimity of the wilderness' in his 1836 essay on American scenery: 'those scenes of solitude from which the *hand of nature has never been lifted* affect the mind with more deep toned emotion than aught which *the hand of man has touched*' (p. 267; emphases added). God's hand sustains wilderness until man's hand spoils it, but, either spiritually or physically, envisioned land is always tactile.

We saw in Cole's *Last of the Mohicans* how unpredictable colonial terrains ravaged by 'improvement' induced antebellum landscape painters to depict sublime visions of storm and flood that anticipate an unstable, multistate, anthropocenic earth, though the cause would have been understood as divine retribution rather than human interference alone. This is why nature continues to thrive after the demise of mankind in *Desolation*, the final painting of the phases of civilization in Coles' *Course of Empire* series (1833–6),

throughout which an 'erratic boulder' surmounts the same mountain peak
(Bedell 2001, 36). Natural Theology explained the unaccountable location of
such boulders, also known as 'perched' boulders or 'rocking' stones (p. 29),
as a vestige of God's superhuman force in breaking up the land and raising
the major mountain chains through Noah's flood. Rebecca Bedell has shown
how Cole and other Hudson River School artists depicted a rocky world
swept by the Deluge that left aqueously rounded forms and U-shaped valleys
littered with erratic boulders, fluvial detritus and evidences of extinction.
Such landscapes signified what the American followers of the British geologists Robert Jameson, William Buckland and William Whewell defined as
catastrophism: short-lived, sudden, violent events where geology harmon-
ized with Genesis in destroying human societies (p. 33).

In other respects, however, geology distanced itself from scriptural inter-
ventions in human affairs. What James Hutton called Gradualism (slow but
continual changes over time) and Charles Lyell called Uniformitarianism
(the present is the key to the past) posited slow geological change over very
long periods that slowly triumphed over catastrophist geology in nineteenth-
century America and elsewhere (Woodward 2014, 23–71) and provided
precedents for Darwinian evolutionary theory in the life sciences. Only
from the 1950s and 1960s onwards did Neocatastrophist theories establish
the coexistence of sudden events of sedimentation and extinction alongside
the gradualist theories of James Hutton and Charles Lyell (Ager 1973), and
only in the 1970s did the discovery of plate tectonics, catastrophic geophys-
ical events, extraterrestrial impacts and the Gaia hypothesis of global inter-
activity prompt geologists to propose a new geological epoch called the
Anthropocene, in which human forces produced abrupt and irreversible
climate change on the same scale as other geomorphic forces (Conceição
et al. 2020).

An apparent split between deep geological and momentary human time
characterizes William Stanley Haseltine's coastal scene *Rocks at Nahant*
(1864), a painting set to refute Marsh's complaint four years earlier that
'few [paintings of] landscapes have a true geographical character' (p. 45). It
was painted in the same year that the Swiss-born professor of natural history
Louis Agassiz lectured in Nahant, Massachusetts, and published cutting-
edge geological theories in an article titled 'Ice-Period in America' (Agassiz
1864; Bedell 2001, 109–21; Pullin 2020, 109–11). Haseltine's painting
shares with Cole's *The Last of the Mohicans* the Lockean quality of tactile,
visual probing but invites us to concentrate on geological time instead of
human history. Geologically informed landscape painters confronted the
problem that while creation narratives carried greater import than those of

merely human history, landscape paintings lacked the dynamic, three-dimensional power of cross-sectional charts and other infographics that Humboldt pioneered in place of words to visualize the causality that structures the earth beneath its surface (Rudwick 1976). As Marsh explained in his review of Humboldt: 'no landscape is a whole'; each one is 'merely the fragmentary contingent resultant of unrelated forces successive in time, discordant in action, and tending to no common aim' (p. 50) of the ideal kind he assumed the art of painting should aspire to. Coastal scenes were at least free of concealing topsoil and foliage, but in *Rocks at Nahant* Haseltine went further by dramatizing the internal energy revealed by the pale 'vein' of frozen magma that traversed the rocks diagonally upwards from the bottom right-hand corner of the painting (**Figure 8**). This vein had been produced by an aggressive intrusion of liquid magma into fractures within horizontal layers of sedimentary gabbro, where it had cooled millennia before (deStefano 2006). Though Agassiz was an idealist catastrophist who believed that the creation was an idea of God, his work illustrates the withdrawal of geological science from scripture, as does Haseltine's, whose flat-top rocks are notably stripped of the detritus that proclaimed the Deluge in Cole's landscapes (Bedell 2001, 119–120). Agassiz knew nothing about the action of tectonic plates but would have understood how veins of molten magma had frozen in the gabbro, how the gabbro had subsequently tilted and fractured it, and how glaciers had accentuated fragmentation, even

Figure 8 William Stanley Haseltine, *Rocks at Nahant,* 1864, oil on canvas, 56.8 × 102.9 cm, Terra Foundation for American Art, Daniel J. Terra Collection, 1999.65

plucking out rock and carrying it away, leaving the extensive inlet in the foreground where the ocean surges in.[4] Marsh had written how a stratum is multicausally 'injected, disjointed, shattered, elevated, tilted' and 'overturned' (1860, pp. 18–19), as we see it has been here.

Erosion has reduced the original site of the image – viewed from Forty Steps Beach towards Castle Rock, Nahant – into a graveyard of its pictured appearance, yet my onsite photograph of 2018 (**Figure 9**) shows that, although almost all the original components of the painting's geology still exist, it is impossible to locate a single viewpoint from which they align with Haseltine's composition. Though the white magma has mostly washed away, the channel that contained it still lines up over several fractures for a considerable distance, but what is missing from the photograph is any evidence of its past or present existence in the prominent slab that occupies the lower right-hand foreground of the painting, where it initiates the main, orthogonal thrust of the perspective. By introducing something that never existed, Haseltine altered the scene to emphasize the magma's puncturing of gabbro layers. In doing so, he transcended the

Figure 9 View toward Castle Rock from Forty Steps Beach, Nahant, Massachusetts, author's photograph, 2018

---

[4] My authority is the geologist Jeffrey D. Vervoort (Washington State University), interviewed 5 April 2018.

literal facts of locality to dramatize the mystery of the vast powers – volcanic and glacial – that operated beneath and above the surface of the rock, both within and beyond the frame of the composition, in which the vein also passes through several, smaller, intra-composition frames formed by fractured planes of rock. The painting seems to ask what unimaginable forces pushed magma through rock, set imponderably heavy slabs on a slant, broke them up and plucked great segments out of them? Departing from exact appearances to visualize the laws of nature in this way resolves the tension between details and ideal forms that worried Marsh and which, more generally (Georgi 2013), American artists inherited from Hazlitt's and Ruskin's battles with Reynolds (see **Section 2** and **5**).

Haseltine wrote that 'everything in nature . . . is worth painting, provided one has discovered the meaning of it. The picture will then tell its own story' (quoted in Bedell 2001, 120). The evidence of the photograph somewhat belies this. The painting tells a story that required alterations to the scene. The manipulation was contrived to endorse the divine providence of Agassiz's geological narrative: 'It would seem that man was intended to decipher the past history of his home' (Agassiz 1864, 92). Like the shattered, once moving hand of a vast geological clock, the white vein identifies us with the tactile forces that formed the rock. Its deep time seemingly contrasts, however, with the transience of crashing waves, scudding yachts and carefree fishermen who pose no threat to the omnipotence of nature, to which they supply human scale befitting incidental staffage in a holiday scene.

Yet it is possible to speculate on a greater significance to these human presences if the artist and his viewers were aware of Agassiz's widely publi-cized theory that racial inferiority was 'a natural fact' (quoted in Yusoff 2020). Agassiz's views on race formation were the outcome of his geological theories (Agassiz 1850, 111). In keeping with the racial paleontologies of his teacher, George Cuvier, and his Uniformitarian rival, Charles Lyell, he subscribed to polygenesis, the belief that God created the races separately and endowed them with different and unequal attributes and aptitudes, as opposed to monogenism, which traces the varieties of mankind back to a common stock epitomized by the Biblical Adam and Eve, from whom 'inferior races' declined due to adverse environmental factors. Ostensibly rejecting politics in favour of science, Agassiz claimed that catastrophes in geological formations caused multiple extinctions of species 'placed' by the Creator in different regions and different points in time for this stern purpose (p. 130). Kathryn Yusoff has explained how he used catastrophic ice ages 'to explain the breaks in genetic relationship of animals and plants from one geologic period to another' and so 'used geologic time to spatialize and hierarchize races in time as either extinct-orientated beings or future orientated beings' (Yusoff 2000). In a hierarchy of racial value that placed native Americans and Africans at the bottom of the scale, only Caucasians could transcend the formative conditions of their places of origin to dominate inferior human species. The evidence of passing glaciers in the painting – what in conscious approximation of geology to art Agassiz called the 'familiar signs, the polished surfaces, the furrows and scratches, the *line-engraving* of the glacier' (1864, 86; his emphasis) – may have served Haseltine as a metaphor of racial cleansing that left behind an 'upper crust' of both social and geological significance.

Perhaps, then, the feelings of 'intense emptiness' arising from the scene (DeLue 2020, 58) is due not to our modern anxiety about ecocide and slavery associated with the American seaboard but rather to a sense of freedom and relief felt by elite holidaymakers, not just from their working lives but from their social and racial inferiors. Likewise, the yachts on the horizon might suggest a commercial or recreational mobility denied to 'othered' races, each of which, in Agassiz's opinion, failed to thrive outside their limited 'biological and zoölogical province' (Agassiz 1850, 134). This was a time when race preoccupied the public mind due to the Emancipation Proclamation, which, two years earlier, had freed the slaves of the Confederate States. In what sense, however, can the tactile activation of the spectator's spatial awareness of the scene be due to remembered associations, in Locke's and Molyneux's sense of the terms, when the vein's intrusion into the gabbro is vastly older even than the passage of the glaciers 15,000 years before? If the painting is intended as anything more than a geologically informed holiday scene, then perhaps the spectators' haptic ride into picture space is due to a primordial identity, subsumed in the creative act of painting, between the providential forces that created the landscape and their '*already being there*' as members of a superior, seaward-looking race manifesting its destiny 'from the inside looking out' (DeLue 2020; her emphasis, 60).

8 Emerson's 'Eye-Ball'

As a subset of natural science, the physiology of human perception relied on theories of origin as much as geology did. Amongst the scrapbooks of the portrait artist Charles Bird King in the Redwood Library at his birthplace, Newport, Rhode Island, there is a beautiful unsigned drawing of an eye, presumably by King himself (**Figure 10**, CBIC.1862.V15.8., in Charles Bird King scrapbook, Redwood Library, Newport, Rhode Island). This rounded, half-opened eye, peculiarly isolated from the rest of the face, might have been a preparatory drawing for a portrait. Perhaps its underlying anatomy was informed by a stray page from a medical textbook scattered with foxing spots in the same archive

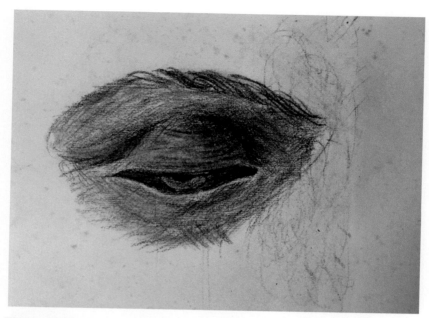

Figure 10 Charles Bird King? Drawing of an eye (c19), CBIC.1862.V15.8., in Charles Bird King scrapbook, Redwood Library, Newport, Rhode Island

(**Figure 11**). It shows cross-sections of an eye within the outline of a human profile by 'H. Anderson, sculpt.'. This must be Hugh Anderson, an American line and stipple engraver and one-time watchmaker based in Philadelphia, whose corpus included landscape views as well as anatomical engravings. Perhaps anatomy stood to this drawing as geology stood to landscape painting, informing its external structure from within, or perhaps King was fascinated by the miracle of the eye itself in view of William Paley's influential comparison between the structures of a watch and the human eye as evidence of purposeful creation in *Natural Theology; or Evidences of the Existence and Attributes of the Deity, Collected from the Appearances of Nature*, a work first published in 1802 that fostered conviction in Intelligent Design on both sides of the Atlantic and remained a standard text at Harvard into the 1850s (Walls 2003, 46). In language whose rhythm aped the cogwheels of Newtonian physics, Paley described 'the series of wheels' in a watch, 'the teeth of which catch in, and apply to, each other, conducting the motion from the fusee to the balance, and from the balance to the pointer' and so on (1815, 8). The eye differs from the watch 'chiefly by surpassing it' in the complexity of its design and the functions it fulfils. How then, he asked, could either mechanism exist 'without a contriver', who in the case of the eye must be the Creator (p. 28)? The eye was the primary example of what still passes today as Intelligent Design.

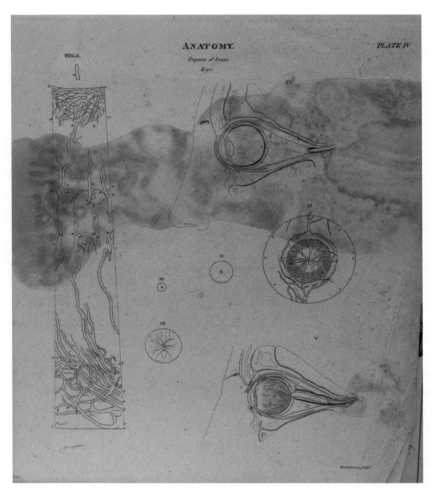

Figure 11 Hugh Anderson, Anatomy. Organs of Sense Eye, plate 4 from an early c19 American reprint, possibly of a c17 anatomy book by Andre Vesalii, found in Charles Bird King's scrapbook, Redwood Library, Newport, Rhode Island

Despite the wide influence on American science of Thomas Reid (Bellion 2011, 28–9), who claimed that the senses had direct access to an external world unmediated by Lockean ideas (Van Cleve 2007), the science of ophthalmology, stimulated by the growing use of spectacles in America (Brownlee 2018), still upheld Locke's and Berkeley's negative answers to Molyneux's question. Thus, in *The Philosophy of the Eye: Being a Familiar Exposition of its Mechanism, and of the Phenomenon of Vision, With a View to Evidence of Design* (1837), a book on optical physiology with an American following (Brownlee 2018, 99,

101, 118), John Walker explained that when an object is examined by the eye, 'the object itself is not seen, paradoxically as it might seem, – it is but the *picture* of the object which is contemplated' (Walker 1837, 19; emphasis added). In a later version of Cheselden's case, in which a Mrs Wardrop is restored to vision by a cataract operation, an orange takes the place of Molyneux's globe, of which 'she could make nothing ... until she actually touched it' (p. 13). Walker concludes that 'an uninstructed eye would be no manner of use to us' and 'that the organ requires as much training or educating, in order to distinguish visual objects as the ear to discriminate sounds' (p. 14) – a thoroughly empiricist answer to the question.

The wealth of optical metaphors in the writings of Ralph Waldo Emerson was probably enriched by his near-complete loss of vision in 1825 due to rheumatic inflammation, which was successfully cured by a surgical procedure not unlike a cataract operation. Something of Paley's mechanistic account of the eye is heard in 'Nature' (1836), the essay that most clearly defined his perceptual outlook. 'By the mutual action of its structure and of the laws of light, perspective is produced, which integrates every mass of objects, of what character soever, into a well coloured and shaded globe, so that where the particular objects are mean and unaffecting, the landscape which they compose, is round and symmetrical' (Emerson 1836, vol. 1, 12). This directly refutes the classical assumption of the flat retina by inflating Locke's 'flat circle variously shadowed' (Locke 1975, 145) into an innately spherical field of vision that turns Paley's mechanistic eye into something that filters out particulars into a preformed artwork.

Throughout the eighteenth century, physiological discoveries concerning binocular vision, focal adjustment, colour and size perception, eye movement, brain connection and species differentiation had continued apace, while in the nineteenth century more systematic investigations under laboratory conditions with scientific instruments such as the stereoscope made fundamental advances in optical understanding (Wade 2005, 73–157; see **Section 10**). Yet by 1811 the Scottish surgeon, anatomist, physiologist, neurologist, artist and philosophical theologian Charles Bell could still conceive of the human eye as of a piece with the rest of divine creation. It did not evolve but was 'formed as it should seem at once in wisdom' (1811, p. 21) without the prior development of mutual reciprocity between animals and the environment on which the development of distinct organs in every species is now known to depend (Land and Nilsson 2012). Yet it is upon such increasingly obsolete assumptions that a different order of perception arose in Emerson's writings, which challenged the stability of perception and opened the gate between human and non-human spheres that the denial of cross-modal relations between touch and vision had closed.

Emerson's essay on 'Nature' concludes with a resoundingly positive answer to Molyneux's question that supplants passive empirical observation with creative spiritual vision in which man triumphs over nature: 'The kingdom of man over nature, *which cometh not with observation* . . . he shall enter without more wonder than *the blind man feels who is gradually restored to perfect sight*' (1836, vol. 1, 45; emphases added). This is but the finale of a quarrel with Locke's theory of perception sustained throughout.

Thus, during the course of the essay Emerson rides two horses, finally jumping from one to the other. He begins by endorsing contemporary science, in which he remained learned throughout his career (Walls 2003). Though he did not discuss the origin of the human eye specifically, by espousing Lyell's gradualist theories he infers that, like the human body that employs it, vision is the product of a long preparation in which geological strata are broken down into soil on which flora and other species thrive to bring it forth (Walls 2003, 92–3). As in 'The Young American', conspicuously heterogeneous factors such as 'the existing state of soils, gases, animals, and morals' conspire to populate the world (Emerson 1844b, vol. 1, 231). But in the seventh chapter on 'Spirit', theological idealism supplants empirical science without rejecting it. Man's material origin in natural history can be conceived of in reverse so that the 'Supreme Being . . . does not build up nature around us, but puts it forth through us' (Emerson 1836, vol. 1, 38). The consequences for perception were outlined in the previous chapter on 'Idealism' where he upheld 'hypothesis of the permanence of nature': the material world stays still enough for science to study it. But the exertions of reason and imagination render the 'outlines and surfaces' of nature 'transparent' so that 'causes and spirits are seen through them' (p. 30). In reaching beyond sensuous phenomena to an unstable and reactive flux of supersensous noumena in this way, Emerson followed Coleridge's error in misconceiving Kantian intuition as 'a nearly mystical perception of precisely those things beyond sensations that Kant had declared inaccessible to human reason' (Boudreau 2013, 104).

Emerson feigned indifference towards the central difference between Locke's materialism and Berkeley's idealism. 'In my utter impotence to test the authenticity of the report of my senses, to know whether the impressions they make on me correspond with outlying objects, what difference does it make whether Orion is up there in heaven, or some god paints the image in the firmament of the soul' (Emerson 1836, vol. 1, 29)? But to call into question the external source of ideas is emphatically to side with Berkeley against Locke, for, alongside Hegel and the Vedanti school of Indian philosophers, Berkeley was the greatest of his philosophical heroes. Emerson had earlier scorned what he regarded as the painstaking empirical task of associating tactile memories with vision in favour of instantaneous and unmediated access to external reality. 'Idealism sees the world in God. It beholds the whole circle of persons and things, of actions and events, of country and religion, not as painfully accumulated, atom after atom, act after act, in an aged creeping Past, but as one vast picture, which God paints on the instant eternity, for the contemplation of the soul' (p. 36). (The resonance here is Macbeth's 'petty pace from day to day'.) But in claiming total, instantaneous access to 'one vast picture', Emerson misconstrued Berkeley, for no less than Locke, Molyneux and perhaps also Kant,[5] Berkeley believed that depth and shape cannot be known from visuals alone.

   Cutting off empiricist roots from spiritual vision and replacing them with idealist philosophy rocked the Boston establishment and caused disputes between the respective protagonists of Locke and Kant in the pages of the New York journals *The Knickerbocker* and *Literary Word* (Stein 1967, 19), but once again theology framed philosophical and aesthetic controversies. Perry Miller argued that the Transcendentalists' 'amateur versions' of idealist philosophy 'were restatements of a native dispensation', by which he means the 'reeling and staggering' of early Quakers intent on flouting 'the intermediacy of Catholic ceremony and ritual' (Miller 1956, 187, 185, 190). It was in a spirit of revival as well as innovation that Emerson resigned his ministry at a Boston church in 1832 to lecture at the Lyceum pulpit, the public education societies spread across the country where he was free from Unitarian scriptural dogma, Newtonian science and Lockean sensational psychology. Although sense and spirit seem opposites to us, Protestant stalwarts such as Jonathan Edwards of the First Awakening saw scientific empiricism and revealed religion as co-dependent because they rooted distant Biblical miracles in the proof of time-bound sensory experience (Brantley 1993, 16). Likewise, the later Unitarians 'were grounded in the philosophy of John Locke and they relied on the five senses: they interpreted Jesus's miracles as sensory, empiricist evidence that his words were revelations from God. As a result, they found the intuitive processes Emerson suggested wholly inadequate for establishing reliable knowledge' (Stula 2008, 19). Emerson's 'Nature', therefore, was an act of apostasy against the sedate Lockean faith in reason prevailing in the Unitarian churches of the wealthy centres of shipping and banking in Boston and Salem (Miller 1956, 193), whose ministers and congregations worried about the insurrectional potential of resurgent 'Enthusiasm', which Locke had denounced in all post-gospel claims concerning miracles: 'he that takes

---

[5] Kant's belief that space was an a priori form of intuition in no way implied that for the newly sighted spatial location was 'homogeneous across the senses'. If Kant had ever tackled Molyneux's question, the jury is still out on what his answer would have been (Sassen 2004, 480).

away *Reason*, to make way for *Revelation*, puts out the Light of both' (Locke 1975, 698; his emphases).

For Emerson, by contrast, all experience was potentially miraculous. Man became God, while nature mirrored the fluctuations of man's soul. In contrast with permanence or gradualism, Emerson conceived of a constant flux (closer to catastrophism) between soul and nature, with one sphere diminishing the other as it enlarged itself, without the filter of a flat retinal image separating consciousness from nature. To prepare the transcendental arguments of the later chapters and closely following the passage on the poetic integration of the landscape inspired by 'a property in the horizon' (see **Section 6**), Emerson famously illustrated the triumph of soul over nature in an experiential account of a miracle towards the beginning of 'Nature'. He had been reading Hazlitt (Scott 2010), and the passage has something of Hazlitt's self-generating narrative reflexivity about it (see **Sections 3** and **4**). 'Crossing a bare common, in snow puddles, at twilight, under a clouded sky', he begins his apocalyptic vision on the horizontal plane with an ordinary winter walk through the woods. His body then morphs into a single eye that rises and expands to comprehend the universe:

> Standing on the bare ground, – my head bathed by the blithe air, and uplifted into infinite space, – all mean egotism vanishes. I become a transparent eyeball. I am nothing. I see all. The currents of the Universal Being circulate through me; I am part or particle of God. The name of the nearest friend sounds then foreign and accidental. To be brothers, to be acquaintances, – master or servant, is then a trifle and a disturbance. I am the lover of uncontained and immortal beauty. In the wilderness, I find something more dear and connate than in streets or villages. In the tranquil landscape, and especially in the distant line of the horizon, man beholds somewhat as beautiful as his own nature. (Emerson 1836, vol. 1, 10)

It has passed unnoticed that the specific inspiration for this passage comes from the Neoplatonic philosophy of a sonnet ('*Ben posson gli occhi* . . . ') by Michelangelo Buonarotti (on whom Emerson wrote an essay) in which the poet beseeches his lady to transform his body into a single eye so that he can behold her face in heaven, since his feet are forbidden to bring his worldly arms and hands where vision can go (Buonarroti 1904, 25). In a careful phonetic analysis of Emerson's passage, Alan Hodder has shown how this vatic eruption shatters the decorum of the walk as 'smooth sentences break and splinter to give way to the rough beast, the intrusive and unsettling apocalypse' (1989, 97). The sentences contract to 'I am nothing. I see all', destroying the ego, filling it with the universe, then emptying it again, before they lengthen again to restore normality.

Throughout this Element we have charted occasions on which paintings of single views expand into worlds or collapse into flatness. Already in the visionary aesthetics of the American artist William Allston, the British trope of collapsed vision persisted in his disapproval of unimaginative spectators for whom Venetian paintings 'will have little more meaning ... than a calico counterpane' (quoted in Bjelejac 1997, 199). As the most extreme of positive responses to Molyneux's question, Emerson's apocalyptic vision proved difficult for artists to visualize. After all, at the climax of the passage the transparent eye-ball lacked an opaque retina for images to form on. 'To see all is to see nothing in particular' (Walls 2003, 100). This is what was lacking in the celebrated semi-comic cartoon of the passage by Emerson's devout follower, Christopher Pearse Cranch, who nevertheless got some things right. The ballooning eye-ball is paradoxically weighted with spindly legs that substitute for arms and hands that spiritual vision has no need of (**Figure 12**). Cranch set the eye-ball in hieratic profile like the Intelligent Design of a Paleyite anatomical drawing, the pigtail doubling as an optic nerve open to the universe (or comically dissected from a brain). Other details are travesties. The ambulatory gaze stalks the landscape a little like Poussin's *Orion*, but it is fixed on clouds, a pervasive symbol of Biblical obscurity in Emerson's oeuvre (Hodder 1989, 95), rather than the infinity of the horizon. Shadows behind the big, flat, unshod feet also challenge infinity with the groundedness of drag marks on solid earth where the eye-ball's stilted stride has ground to a halt. The sporting hat and formal coat and tails evoke the genteel poverty of a barefoot missionary or ambient lecturer within a domesticated, middle landscape that hardly amounts to 'wilderness'. The humour resides in the fantastical incredibility of such an event ever befalling a mere mortal, but Cranch loses the Transcendental resonance, just as his serious paintings largely fail to express spirituality unless an expert explains their symbolism (Stula).

Despite the difficulties of visualising Emerson's spiritually disembodied language, perhaps his uplifting idealism anchors the all-seeing, hovering eye that confronts the abyss of Frederick Church's *The Andes of Ecuador* (1855). Perhaps too his claim that 'the health of the eye seems to demand a horizon' is the impetus behind many American wilderness scenes that furnish distant access for the eye but not for the body across impenetrable vegetation, precipices, and mountains (Emerson 1836, vol. 1, 13). In Durand's *Kindred Spirits* (1849) our eyes shoot out over vast distances, stranding tactility, while in Church's Turnerian *Cotopaxi* (1869), the strong directional forces of natural phenomena such as waterfalls, rivers, and volcano smoke restrain the viewer from all but visual entry into picture space. Such terrains appear trackless even for the lone Indigenous observers often planted in them as symbols of primitive

Figure 12 Christopher Pearse Cranch, *Standing on the Base Ground ...
I Become a Transparent Eyeball* (illustration for Ralph Waldo Emerson's
'Nature'), 1830–2, pen and ink, 21.3 × 14.4 cm, Metropolitan Museum of
Art, Gift of Whitney Dall, Jr., in Memory of Emily Dall, 1976,
1976.625.20(1)

worlds (despite their indispensable local knowledge as guides). While the Lockean formation of national character required topographical specificity that was hard for settlers to picture in the unvariegated terrains of supposedly untouched Nature, Emerson thought that 'we are never tired, so long as we can see far enough' (p. 13). The infinity implied by the blurred horizons of later paintings by George Innes, whose spiritual aesthetics are explicitly predicated on Molyneux's question, performs variations on this (DeLue 2004, 3–4, 50–7, 103, 106).

Emerson wrote that the painter 'should know that landscape has beauty for his eye ... because the same power which sees through his eyes ... is seen in that spectacle' (Emerson 1971–2013, vol. 2, 209). The heady feedback loop by which the universe courses through his apocalyptic eye in 'Nature' implies a forward-facing fusion that recycles Ruskin's 'natural tendency impressed on us by our Creator to love the forms ... out of which He formed our bodies' (1851, vol. 9, 271). But if idealism permits our frontally located eyes to eliminate barriers between soul and matter, how does it overcome physical constraints to lateral, all-round vision such as the capacity to see the world behind us or what is behind what we can see? Emerson's first encounter with Berkeleyan immaterialism had made the physical world 'oscillate a little & threaten to dance' (1939, vol. 2, 384). The tremor increased in 'Nature' when failures of empathy induced visual opacity because 'the axis of vision is not coincident with the axis of things' (1836, vol. 1, 43). But in the essay on 'Circles', spirit takes over from nature, encapsulating and ensphering the universe through a mystical radiation of concentric circles of which 'the eye is the first ... ; the horizon which it forms is the second', while around every further circle 'another can be drawn' ad infinitum (1841, vol. 2, 179). Thus, 'the natural world may be conceived of as a system of concentric circles, and we now and then detect in nature slight dislocations, which apprize us that this surface on which we now stand, is not fixed, but sliding' (p. 186).

These lateral dislocations were far from slight in Fitz Henry Lane's *Brace's Rock, Brace's Cove* (1864), a painting untypical of his own work and of the so-called Luminist painting it is classed with. Lane was on a register of a Boston-based organization of the American Union of Associationists, which sought to unite Transcendentalism with social reform. From 1848 Emerson was active in the Gloucester Lyceum where Lane was 'probably directly involved in contracting him to speak' between 1850 and 1863 (Foley 1995–6, 99–100), the year before the picture that concerns us was painted. Based on a field study (*Brace's Rock, Eastern Point*, 1863), Lane's painting of Brace's Rock near Gloucester largely relinquished the practical focus of an artist who had hitherto 'earned his money ... mostly by painting "portraits" of vessels for

Figure 13 Fitz Henry Lane, *Brace's Rock, Brace's Cove*, 1864, oil on canvas, 26 × 38.7 cm, Terra Foundation for American Art, Danie J. Terra Collection, 1999.83

sails and ship-owners', as the art critic Clarence Cook wrote (1854, 308). This painting (**Figure 13**) was probably the last of two other paintings also based on the field study, which varied in the position and angle of the boat but otherwise followed the field study quite closely, remaining faithful to the scene for locals, mariners and holiday makers who would have recognized it. Like the others, it was a haunting twilight scene of a notoriously dangerous group of rocks viewed from a cove near Lane's home in Gloucester, Massachusetts, where gently lapping waves and a skeletal, foreboding-looking small boat disrupt the otherwise placid seascape. The series reflected the bleak outlook of a nation devastated by the Civil War (1861–5), when shipwrecked vessels became a common artistic metaphor for the battles raging between North and South. This picture is an anomaly, however, deviating mysteriously from the originating sketch and from the actual topography. While retaining a familial resemblance to the other paintings based on the field study, it offers a mirror image of their topography: the rock appears to show what would be its back when viewed from the cove and sits on the left rather than the right. Emerson had proclaimed in 'Nature' that the poet 'unfixes the land and sea, makes them revolve around the axis of his primary thought, and disposes them anew. Possessed himself by a heroic passion, he uses matter as symbols of it' (1836 vol. 1, p. 30). This appears to happen here.

A slowly swinging, Hogarthian line of beauty marks the route by which the wrecked boat must have landed. Its mast cuts across this passageway and the tonally contrasting layers of rock and sea, energizing the tranquil scene whose horizon is lower, and sky larger, than in earlier iterations. The beached hull – crack-ribbed but still masted – defies easy explanation as a symbol: if wrecked at sea, how did it find its way to these placid sands, whose foreground is marked by autumnal foliage? If abandoned, how had it not washed out to sea? The listing mast seems to radiate a force field, driving ripples of the ebbing tide into widening concentric ellipses, like waves from a radio tower or like the 'system of concentric circles' rushing 'on all sides outwards to new and larger circles' in Emerson's 'Circles' (1841, vol. 2, 186, 180).

The point of intersection between mast and horizon fixes the viewer's sight line, but where is the viewer standing? Locals would know that this side of the rock could only be seen from the shore south of the cove, where granite cliffs plunge into the sea with no place for an observing painter to stand (**Figure 14**). Ten years earlier Clarence Cook had described Lane as 'a man apparently of forty years, walking with difficulty, supported by crutches' (1854, p. 307). He was now in his final year. Following reports of this precarious viewpoint (Holdsworth n.d.), I scrambled over this terrain in 2018. Another photograph of the route to these cliffs shows how unlikely it is that a severely handicapped

Figure 14 View of Brace's Cove, author's photograph, 2018

Figure 15 View of Brace's Cove, author's photograph, 2018

man could have obtained this view of the rock (**Figure 15**), except by boat, which the painting disallows. Yet only something like tall cliffs could explain the prolonged shadow stretching to the globular rosary of apparently diluvial boulders and reflections in the middle distance: a dark brown spit engulfed by the cold yellow reflection of Brace's Rock as real as the Rock itself – a fractured leviathan, enlarged, reversed, and upside down beneath the duck-egg blue sky. The philosopher Maurice Merleau-Ponty contended that 'if we abandon the empiricist premise that privileges the content of perception, we are free to acknowledge the strange mode of existence of the world behind us' (2002, 29). But in Emerson's 'Nature', Lane already had available the source of a similar idea from Plato's cave: nature 'always speaks of spirit. It suggests the absolute. ... It is a great shadow always pointing to the sun behind us' (p. 37). Spinning Brace's Rock around, effacing the difference between reflections and their sources, making us aware of the world behind the artist from a point where he could not stand – might this not all have been an aspiration to total vision, to impossible consciousness of the world bathed in crystalline light as it might have existed beyond death for a non-existent observer, a total surrounding that encompassed the visual presence of the other side of what is before us and that which is behind us? In fusing contradictory views, Lane's self-effacing, gyroscopic vision invokes an impossible post-mortem perception:

a once-familiar world from which the artist and his point of view are absent. Only the memento mori of the skeletal wreck is left to intimate the intrusion of a world beyond into a place where human life is extinct.

If so, then in other respects this eerie apocalyptic scene departs from the optimistic and progressive tendency in Emerson's thought, which enlarged rather than eliminated self almost to the point of solipsism. Indeed, he significantly intensified an 'anthropocentric shift' by substituting the creative mind of man for God the Creator (Bilbro 2015, 3–4), while fully complying with the commandments of Genesis to 'fill the earth and subdue it; have dominion over the fish of the sea and the birds of the air, and over every living thing that lives on earth' (I, 28), a passage that justified the entire colonial project. For the Hudson River School of painters, the colonial pursuit of Manifest Destiny vied with an Old Testament view of the universe in which the human soul was either enlarged by faith or dwarfed by greed (Veith 2001, 58–61, 70–6, 94, 99, 116–19), but their inclusion of human figures 'shrunk almost to nothingness as they confront an objective order that they can neither control nor fully grasp' (p. 59) would have smacked too much of fallen humanity for Emerson, for whom 'man is the dwarf of himself' (1836, vol 1, 43) when he fails to fulfil his destiny. Despite embracing the abolition of slavery and other progressive social policies consistent with the political and moral aims of the French and American revolutions, Emerson applauded colonial expansionism and industrial progress (Walls 2003, 105), imagining how nature welcomed the heroic arrival of Columbus. 'Does not the New World clothe his form with her palm-groves and savannahs as fit drapery' (1836, vol. 1, 15)? In 'The Poet' 'nature adopts' 'the factory village and the railway' 'very fast into her vital circles, and the gliding train of cars she loves like her own', for they 'fall within the great Order' (1844a, vol. 3, 11). Thus, the God-like view over prospective colonial territory in Church's *The Andes of the Ecuador* (1855) and the vector described by the steaming locomotive arcing around the railway viaduct in Jasper Francis Cropsey's *Starrucca Valley* (1856) would both have been within the remit of Emerson's spiritual optics.

Berkeley himself may have exerted an older idealist influence on a later generation of artists working in the 1850s and 1860s around Newport, Rhode Island, a region that had gained the reputation of a 'philosophical landscape' as a result of his presence there between 1729 and 1731 when revising aspects of his theories of vision in *Alciphron: Or the Minute Philosopher* (1731) and awaiting funds that never came to establish an impractical mission in the Bermuda Islands. He was accompanied by the artist John Smibert, who may have been the first to propagate his ideas on vision in American landscape painting (O'Donnell 2017). The horizontal bands of landscape in the works of

John Frederick Kensett, Sanford Robinson Gifford and Martin Johnson Heade
tended to resolve into spatial wholeness without the dramatic thrust of Hudson
River School paintings but with a slight delay of spatial recognition that
decoupled them from material appearances. This prefigured a partially autonomous realm of art as wilderness moved westward from the civilized landscapes
preferred by urban elite vacationers whose interests were shifting from geology
to Darwinian controversies in the life sciences. I have argued elsewhere that
such a delay may derive from Berkeley's conception of the blind man restored
to vision who would construe visual signs in the faltering way a non-native
speaker might construe a second language (Read 2020, 135–7). In transcending
scientific concerns in favour of places of the mind designed for aesthetic
dreaming, where ethnic and environmental conflicts are firmly relegated outside
the frame, these painters reflect a larger 'critical shift' towards aestheticism in
America (Georgi 2013, 76–109), which falls beyond the scope of this Element.

9 Mixed Answers: Australia

Australian landscape painting plays a minor role in this Element because it
lacked engagement with one of the perceptual theories I have been tracing. In
the service of British empire, almost every early Australian image discussed in
Bernard Smith's *European Vision and the South Pacific* (1965) clove to the
empiricist tradition of scientific realism established by Captain James Cook's
painter William Hodges, who abandoned authority based on classical landscape
in favour of 'compositional elements . . . determined not by reference to states of
mind but by reference to the interrelation of the facts and scientific laws
determining the nature of a given environment' (Smith 1960, 51). Idealist
philosophy, by contrast, did not take root in Australia until the establishment
of universities from the 1850s onward. Even then, since Australia did not gain
national independence until 1907, it tended to concentrate on the role of
Hegelian spirit in the task of nation-building rather than the metaphysical
idealism of Berkeley and Kant (Hughes-Warrington and Tregenza 2008).

  Yet there was a pronounced Romanticism in the work of many English artists
freshly arrived in Australia. Partly due to its extreme length against height, and
partly due to the flicker of analogies and differences in the shapes of its white
clouds, green bush, yellow beaches and striated blue-green waters of its inlet,
there is an exhilarating expansiveness to Thomas Turner's pen-and-ink watercolour of apparently virgin bush (**Figure 16**). On first impression we might
think we are looking at the first explorers of a potentially endless shoreline in an
unspoilt Arcadia. Another picturesque quality is that Turner enclosed other
watercolours of the same view in compressed oval frames that recall Gilpin's

Figure 16 Thomas Turner, *Augusta Hardy's Inlet: First Settlement, May 1830,* pen and ink and watercolour, 17.1 × 41.4 cm (trimmed sheet), State Art Collection, Art Gallery of Western Australia, gift of Mr J. R. Turner, 1929

illustrations in *Observations on the River Wye*. Drawings in the State Library of Western Australia Turner made before leaving England attest to his picturesque interest in dilapidated houses and broken fences. Though he was only sixteen on reaching the richly forested wilderness surrounding Hardy's Inlet, Western Australia, in 1830 with other members of James Turner's family, he seems to have received good training from his English boarding school and perhaps from his father, a successful London builder, surveyor and accomplished architectural artist. We may doubt whether Thomas had read Locke, but there are many tactile associations in the construction of his picture space. The slowly trudging men who haul the raft as another steers on board provide traction that propels the eye up the smooth sand of the vertically rising beach that lies ahead. Also tactile is the way in which the entire shoreline has been lassoed and tilted upwards with a centrifugal force that splays the trees out on the left where the beach is widest. It tautens the soft sand geology of the circumambient shore-lines. Locals I have spoken to at Augusta insist on the sketch's accuracy, and indeed the rocks just ahead of the raft are still there (**Figure 17**), but I was unable to find a standpoint high enough to encompass the whole view, which, however characteristic of the area, is closer to a mental map or survey. With a slightly military air, the black shape of a rowing boat receding at an angle beats another track into space, for the scene is not unpeopled at all.

On close inspection the white pyramidal boulders half-hidden in the mela-leuca trees on the left are tents to which the raft brings supplies. There is already a cluster of goods on the adjacent beach, for Turner is not recording a moment but a laborious, oft-repeated process in a painting of heroic origins, as confirmed by the subtitle, *First Settlement May 1930,* and by other paintings of intermediary clearance culminating in *Albion House, Augusta, After Clearing of Land*

Figure 17 Rocks on Seine Bay foreshore, Augusta, author's photograph, 2020

Figure 18 Thomas Turner, *Albion House, Augusta, After Clearing of Land*, c1840s, pen, ink and watercolour, 14.1 × 27.8 cm, State Art Collection, Art Gallery of Western Australia, Gift of Mr J. R. Turner, 1929

(**Figure 18**) where the linear fences of the farmstead almost engulf the inlet as if it were an extra paddock and neat furrows radiate outwards towards the spectator. The triumph of physical exertion over nature is complete. As opposed to the Gilpinesque oval framing of other paintings, the rectilinear format of *First Settlement May 1930* betrays highly utilitarian, indeed military, connotations, since the development of the panoramic sketch by Paul Sandby as taught in eighteenth-century military academies was a highly effective means of asserting authority over alien terrains (Gooding 2007, 69). What dangers warranted military protection may be revealed by blackened trees retaining foliage on the left. In other watercolours of the same scene there is no blackening there, so it does not represent a change of tone or species. The cause may be controlled burns by the Wardandi people conducted in manageable clusters during winter so that foliage would be ready to grow again in the right season. Relations between local tribes and the three settler families in the area slowly deteriorated during the 1830s, and eventually Turnwood, one of the Turners' properties, was destroyed by fire, probably as a result of this necessary, age-old custom. The government's withdrawal of the garrison from Augusta was a crucial reason for James Turner abandoning Augusta in 1850 after Thomas had moved to the protected region of the Vasse in 1840 (Turner 1956, p. 118). The Romantic picturesqueness of *First Settlement* is not altogether fugitive, however. Its unspoiled beauty expressed the ambitions of landed gentlemen forbidden to London artisans. The sketch was synoptic rather than exact, because, although it remained in the family's possession in Australia, it was probably made to impress those who, unlike Haseltine and Lane's clients, had never seen the scene. As James Turner wrote to his eldest brother in London in 1831: 'We have a fine prospect down the River & you may expect [at] the first opportunity to receive faithful sketches from nature of our new country' (1956, p. 78).

If Thomas Turner's work is nevertheless typical of Australian empirical vision, future research may discover whether Australian artists gleaned currents of idealism from well-informed patrons, literary luminaries, religious activists and well stocked libraries earlier in the century (Dixon 1986, 2–4). Certainly, Australia's first literary patron, Nicol Drysdale Stenhouse, a friend of Thomas De Quincey's who arrived from Scotland in 1838, disseminated Kantian and American Transcendentalist ideas in Sydney during the 1850s and 1860s, but his circle apparently contained no artists (Jordens 1979, 24, 46–8, 95–6, 124–5). It is more likely that idealist theories came to the visual arts through the 'Düsseldorf effect' (Pullin 2020), to which many American and Australian artists were subject in the early nineteenth century. As Ruth Pullin argues, given his interests, tastes in reading, and the circles in which he moved in Germany and Melbourne, Düsseldorf-trained artist Eugene von Guérard was almost certainly familiar with most of Alexander von Humboldt's works. His *Cosmos* betrays many idealist assumptions embedding consciousness in nature. In contrast to the military uses of panoramic representation, Humboldt advocated the construction of panoramic buildings to increase the public's 'conception of the natural unity and the feeling of the harmonious accord pervading the

Figure 19 Eugene von Guérard, *View of Tower Hill,* 1855, oil on canvas, Warrnambool Art Gallery, Victoria (on loan from the Department of Sustainability and Environment), gift of Mrs E. Thornton, 1966

Figure 20 Tower Hill Reserve, Victoria, author's photograph, 2017

universe' (1948–52, vol. 2, 457). It is an idealist conception that furnished a rare example of environmental empathy in landscape painting.

On visiting von Guérard's *View of Tower Hill* (1855; **Figure 19**) at the Warrnambool Art Gallery in Victoria, I discovered it was only possible to capture a semblance of the painting at its nearby site, Tower Hill Reserve, by putting my camera on the panorama setting (**Figure 20**). In *View of Tower Hill* we sense von Guérard's identification with the idealism of Humboldt's panoramic idea in how he interpolates the spectator into a felt unity of curvilinear space that captures the geological dynamism of the volcanic terrain. While distilling Humboldt's wholist conception of landscape as the work of the Creator, however, von Guérard scatters sharp focal points about the scene to trigger erratic redirections of the gaze as it refocuses on loosely connected, even unrelated groups of creatures – Indigenous people, kangaroos, ducks and flocks of birds – moving in different directions at different speeds. These effects are remarkably consistent with Humboldt's empirical theory of the 'outness' and tactile motility of vision in *Über Denken und Sprechen* (1801), gleaned from a close reading of Étienne Bonnot de Condillac's *Traité des sensations* (1754), which revolutionized Humboldt's thought (Aarslef and Logan 2016, 770).

At first Condillac had joined British and continental philosophers who had offered positive answers to Molyneux's question, but in *Traité des sensations* he changed his mind (Aarslef and Logan 2016, 768–81). In a famous thought experiment, he successively endowed a statue with the senses of smell, hearing, taste and vision, denying that any of them would furnish any understanding of an outer world and so gain any corresponding awareness of self. Only with the introduction of touch did the statue escape solipsism and gain consciousness (Condillac cited by Morgan 1977, 72–79). Touch, therefore, becomes the teacher of the other senses by providing a form of attention through which the rest learn to make, as Humboldt understood him, 'analogical inferences' (translated by Aarselff and Logan 2016, 771). In the 1798 edition of the treatise, Condillac crucially added movement to his observations on touch, an amplification that Humboldt registered and recognized (Aarselff and Logan 2016, 771). Tactile awareness of spatial movement is conferred on the eyes when objects appear to break away from one another within the field of vision. Condillac thus defined a cross-modal consciousness that was *equivalent* to positive answers to Molyneux's question.

Von Guérard's paintings invite both profound reverie at overall effect and shifting focus on detail. They give an impression of tremendous volatility in the eye's attention to nascent movements in manifold life forms and weather systems within a geologically dynamized landscape. This is their main difference from, say, the stasis of Frederick Church's *Andes of Ecuador* (1855) in which the observer is obliged to cut up wholes into details through a sharpening focus akin to scientific dissection (Raab 2015, 67). *View of Tower Hill* is not a primordial scene, for sailing ships on the horizon harmonize with evidence of other living creatures in a painting that respected the landowner's pastoral interests without decentring the rest of creation living off the environment that envelops it. A sense of the observer's freedom to change focus in following creatures that move of their own volition seems to coexist with the iron-clad dictates of divine destiny. Though von Guérard would likely have sided with Humboldt in Condillac's negative answer to Molyneux's question, his paintings seem to fuse idealism and empiricism. Few paintings have had more benevolent effects on the environments they represent. *View of Tower Hill* was commissioned by James Dawson, a leading preservationist, champion of Aboriginal rights, and defender of animal rights. He protested when the site deteriorated from the pristine health depicted in von Guérard's painting, which, after Tower Hill became Australia's first national park, served as a model for restoring it to its original condition. It is now again under Aboriginal management (Bonyhady 2003, 339–66).

10 Conclusion

The classical assumption of the flat retinal image persisted in twentieth-century mainstream aesthetics in Bernard Berenson theory of 'tactile values' and Roger Fry's theory of 'Significant Form', which reached them through the German aesthetics of Conrad Fiedler, Adolf Hildebrand and Heinrich Wölfflin (Clark 1956, 235): the artist can only accomplish his task of conveying pictorial reality 'by giving tactile values to retinal impressions' (Berenson 1908, 4). This was a proposition devised for Florentine Renaissance paintings that Clement Greenberg specifically revoked in championing the flatness of abstract art in 1960: 'The Old Masters created an illusion of space in depth that one could imagine oneself walking into, but the analogous illusion created by the Modernist painting can only be seen into; can be travelled through, literally or figuratively, only with the eye' (Greenberg 1993, 90). It was in Germany also in 1867 that the battle between empiricism and idealism for control over the flat retinal image was superseded by Hermann von Helmholtz's nativist-empiricist controversy in which visual perception was defined as 'quasi-inferential' in character, occurring 'high in the central nervous system rather than in the end-organs', as his empiricist rival Karl Ewald Konstantin Hering had contended (Turner 1993, 177). For Helmholtz, spatial orientation is learned by cross-checking algorithmically against the mental image so that perception is experienced as immediate when in fact it is projected according to the laws and needs of the nervous system (p. 185).

Molyneux's question lives on in contemporary philosophy and cognitive neuroscience not as one question but as many (Glenny 2013b; Matthen and Cohen 2020), as Denis Diderot had anticipated in the eighteenth-century (Morgan 1977, 25–58). In an experiment designed to establish an answer to the question based on scientific criteria, Richard Held and his colleagues found that, as their title states, 'the newly sighted fail to match seen with felt' (Held et al. 2011). After operations on subjects aged between eight and seventeen from underdeveloped countries, this negative answer was partially qualified by the subjects' ability to identify objects through separate sense organs 'after short real-world experiences' (p. 552), yet their vision remained severely impaired, as it would have been for Cheselden's patient. Pawan Sinha, however, speculated on a dialectical relationship between positive and negative answers in which visual learning from experience may be innately determined: 'some amount of structure in the visual pathway is laid down by the genomic information that the nervous system is using in order to pattern itself. ... And then the finer grain connectivity will be modified by the actual visual experience' (Johnson 2020). Held et al., also speculated that this learning component may have an ecological basis in allowing for bodily growth and adjustment to new objects and environments (2011, p. 522).

In broader cultural terms, today's assumptions about sensory perception are remote from the tradition of immediate two-dimensional vision and its idealist alternatives. The richly multisensorial concreteness of Maurice Merleau-Ponty's phenomenology, popular with art students in search of a theorist, aligns with contemporary sensibilities. He posited proactive attention to objects whose simultaneously accessible, multisensorial qualities nevertheless appear to materialize outside us (Merleau-Ponty 2002, 271). 'In the jerk of the twig from which a bird has just flown, we read its flexibility or elasticity and it is thus that a branch of an apple-tree or a birch are immediately distinguishable' (p. 267). In the long section on 'The Senses' in *The Phenomenology of Perception* (1945), he mounted a major assault on the premises and consequences of Molyneux's question, convicting it of the cardinal error of the Cartesian-Lockean scientific tradition: unbinding the unity of the body's openness to the environmental field from which sensory perception evolved. Far from denying the different characteristics of each sensory field, he argued that each has its own spatial character that admits visual characteristics: 'indeed the unity of space can be discovered only in the interplay of the sensory realms' (p. 258). Thus, the effort to separate the senses, as required by the hypothesis of the flat retinal image, 'assumes a highly particularized attitude' (p. 84). On this view the seventeenth-century philosophers and their subsequent interlocutors had it back to front in starting with the separation of the senses as means of understanding the mind's access to the world. Rather, the unified field of perception is the prerequisite of deliberate and highly specialized attempts to segregate the senses, one of which is planar vision and its representation (Gibson 1951, 404–5).

Many commentators have granted universal validity to these eloquent, participatory aspects of Merleau-Ponty's theories, as if it accorded privileged understanding of the animistic relationship with nature that Indigenous peoples enjoyed before colonial occupation. With Merleau-Ponty in mind, for example, David Abram reflected that 'prior to all our verbal reflections, at the level of our

spontaneous, sensorial engagement with the world around, we are *all* animals'
(1997, 57; his emphasis). Attractive as this vicarious inhabitation of primordial
bodies may seem, its predication on a self-enclosed solitary encounter looking
outward from a centre on the unified prospect of the world claims false
knowledge of sensory encounters filtered by the collective memories of
Indigenous people interacting with each other over millennia (Hamilakis
2011, 211). Primitivist assumptions may also underpin the claim that the
colonizing vision of landscape painting went missing from native cultures
because their land was 'never alien enough to need representation' until their
peoples were removed from it (Ash-Milby 2007, 23). But even were it true that
Western landscape painting has always been concerned with power relations
rather than intimate oneness with nature, symbolic mapping of social, geographical and cosmological relations has always been widely practised in
Indigenous cultures.

What rings true about Merleau-Ponty's attack on empirical answers to
Molyneux's question is that their perceiving subject 'describes sensations
and their substratum as one might describe the fauna of a distant land' (2002,
240). Michel Foucault also correlated 'the foreign spectator in an unknown
country and the man born blind restored to sight' as 'the two great mythical
experiences' on which Enlightenment philosophy based its premises (1973,
65). I have tried to show that the scientific questions raised by Molyneux's
question are entrenched in perceptions of European colonial ambition. The
resulting transformations of newly conquered territories are predicated upon
the sensory coordination of pre-emptive possession rehearsed in landscape
paintings, which allocate values across the spectra of soul and body, mind
and matter, wilderness and cleared land, settlers and indigenes. I have argued
that Molyneux's question was not merely a formative element in colonial
landscape aesthetics but was itself the product of colonial imagining. In
questioning the relations between what is seen and what is touched, it helped
transport minds to distant places and empirically control them. Though
idealist theories challenged the moral bankruptcy of scientific materialism,
they encouraged human ascendency over nature that quickened the
Anthropocene. Predicated on positive answers, the flight of the eye beyond
the limits of the body propelled the speeding bullet and put artists at the
forefront of railway, tourist and urban development inspired by easel paintings of inaccessible natural wonders. Molyneux's question lives on in the
human–machine interface of sensory substitution and stem cell research
based on a vastly greater sense of brain neuroplasticity (Glenney 2013a;
Makin 2019; Eagleman 2021). While providing hope for the blind, the wider
consequences of trans-modal technology remain to be seen. In Wally

Pfister's film *Transcendence* (2014), the pincers of an unimaginable future technology slide into the cranium of a blinded man to restore his vision but subordinate his freedom to a global corporation, the online version of Berkeley's God, supplying three-dimensional consciousness the physical senses cannot muster.

References

Aarsleff, Hans, and John L. Logan (2016). An Essay on the Context and Formation of Wilhelm von Humboldt's Linguistic Thought. *History of European Ideas* 42(6), 768–71.

Abram, David (1997). *The Spell of the Sensuous: Perception and Language in a More-Than-Human World*. New York: Vintage Books.

Addison, Joseph (1710). Essays on the Pleasure of the Imagination. In vol. 3 of Donald F. Bond, ed. (1965), *The Spectator*, 5 vols, pp. 535–82. Oxford: Oxford University Press.

Agassiz, Jean Louis Rodolphe (1850). The Diversity of Origin of the Human Races. *Christian Examiner* 49, 110–45.

Agassiz, Jean Louis Rodolphe (1864). Ice-Period in America. *Atlantic Monthly* 14(81), 86–93.

Ager, Derek V. (1973). *The Nature of the Stratigraphic Record*. New York: Halsted Press.

Alison, Archibald (1790). *Essays on the Nature and Principles of Taste*. London: J. J. G. and G. Robinson; Edinburgh: Bell and Bradfute.

Anstey, Peter R., and Albert Vanzo (2019). Introduction. In Peter R. Anstey and Albert Vanzo, eds., *Experiment, Speculation and Religion in Early Modern Philosophy*, pp. 1–7. London: Taylor & Francis.

Arneil, Barbara (1996). The Wild Indian's Venison: Locke's Theory of Property and English Colonialism in America. *Political Studies* 44(1), 60–74.

Ash-Milby, Kathleen (2007). The Imaginary Landscape. In *Off the Map: Landscape in the Native Imagination*, ed. Kathleen Ash Milby, pp. 17–45. Washington, DC: National Museum of the American Indian, Smithsonian Institution.

Barrell, John (1972). *The Idea of Landscape and the Sense of Place 1730–1840: An Approach to the Poetry of John Clare*. Cambridge: Cambridge University Press.

Barringer, Tim (1994). The Englishness of Thomas Cole. In Alan Wallach and William H. Truettner, eds., *Thomas Cole: Landscape into History* pp. 1–51. New Haven, CT: Yale University Press; Washington, DC: National Museum of American Art, Smithsonian Institution.

Barringer, Tim, and Elizabeth Mankin Kornhauser (2018). *Thomas Cole's Journey: Atlantic Crossings*. New York: Metropolitan Museum.

Bedell, Rebecca (2001). *The Anatomy of Nature, Geology & American Landscape Painting, 1825–1875*. Princeton, NJ: Princeton University Press.

Bedell, Rebecca (2018). *Moved to Tears: Rethinking the Art of the Sentimental in the United States*. Princeton, NJ: Princeton University Press.

Bjelejac, David (1997). *Washington Allston, Secret Societies, and the Alchemy of Anglo-American Painting*. Cambridge: Cambridge University Press.

Bell, Charles (1811). The New Anatomy of the Brain. In William N. Dember, ed. (1864), *Visual Perception: The Nineteenth Century*, pp. 18–32. New York: John Wiley & Sons.

Bellion, Wendy (2011). *Citizen Spectator: Art, Illusion and Visual Perception in Early National America*. Chapel Hill: University of North Carolina Press.

Berenson, Bernard (1908). *The Florentine Painters of the Renaissance*, 3rd ed. London: G. P. Putnam's Sons.

Berkeley, George (1709). *An Essay Towards a New Theory of Vision*. In Desmond M. Clark, ed. (2008), *George Berkeley: Philosophical Writings*, pp. 1–66. Cambridge: Cambridge University Press.

Berkeley, George (1710). *A Treatise Concerning the Principles of Human Knowledge*. In Desmond M. Clark, ed. (2008), *George Berkeley: Philosophical Writings*, pp. 67–150. Cambridge: Cambridge University Press.

Berkeley, George (1732). *Alciphron, or the Minute Philosopher*. In Desmond M. Clark, ed. (2008), *George Berkeley: Philosophical Writings*, pp. 269–314. Cambridge: Cambridge University Press.

Berkeley, George (1733). *The Theory of Vision, or Visual Language, Shewing the Immediate Presence and Providence of a Deity, Vindicated and Explained*. London: J. Tonson.

Berman, David (2009). *Berkeley and Irish Philosophy*. London: Continuum.

Bilbro, Jeffrey (2015). *Loving God's Wildness: The Christian Roots of Ecological Ethics in American Literature*. Tuscaloosa: University of Alabama Press.

Bonyhady, Tim (2003). *The Colonial Earth*. Melbourne: Melbourne University Press.

Boudreau, Kristin (2013). Human Mind. In Wesley T. Mott, ed., *Ralph Waldo Emerson in Context*, pp. 101–8. Cambridge: Cambridge University Press.

Brantley, Richard E. (1993). *Coordinates of Anglo-American Romanticism: Wesley, Edwards, Carlyle and Emerson*. Gainesville: University of Florida Press.

Bromwich, David (1983). *Hazlitt: The Mind of a Critic*. Oxford: Oxford University Press.

Brownlee, Peter John (2008). Manifest Destiny/Manifest Responsibility. In Peter John Brownlee, ed., *Manifest Destiny/Manifest Responsibility: Environmentalism and the Art of the American Landscape*, pp. 23–33. Chicago, IL: Terra Foundation for American Art.

Brownlee, Peter John (2018). *The Commerce of Vision: Optical Culture and Perception in Antebellum America*. Philadelphia: University of Pennsylvania Press.

Budge, Gavin (2008). The Hero as Seer: Character, Perception and Cultural Health in Carlyle. *Romanticism and Victorianism on the Net*, 52, https://doi.org/10.7202/019805ar.

Buonarroti, Michael Angelo (1904). *The Sonnets of Michael Angelo Buonarroti*, trans. J. A. Symonds, 2nd ed. London: Smith Elder & Co.; New York: Charles Scribner's Sons.

Cassirer, Ernst (1951). *The Philosophy of the Enlightenment*, trans. C. A. Koelin and J. P. Pettegrove. Princeton, NJ: Princeton University Press.

Catlin, George (1995). *Letters and Notes on the North American Indians*, 2 vols. North Dighton, MA: JG Press.

Chase, Stanley P. (1924). Hazlitt as a Critic of Art. *Publications of the Modern Languages Association* 39(1), 179–202.

Cheselden, William (1728). An Account of some Observations made by a young Gentleman, who was born blind, or lost his Sight so early, that he had no Remembrance of ever having seen, and was couch'd between 13 and 14 Years of Age. *Philosophical Transactions of the Royal Society of London* 7, 447–50, https://royalsocietypublishing.org/doi/pdf/10.1098/rstl.1727.0038.

Clark, Kenneth (1956). The Study of Art History. *Higher Education Quarterly* 10(3), 223–38.

Cole, Thomas (1836). Essay on American Scenery. In Sarah Burns and John Davis, eds. (2009). *American Art to 1900: A Documentary*, pp. 264–71. Berkeley: University of California Press.

Cole, Thomas (1980). *Thomas Cole: The Collected Essays and Prose Sketches*, ed. Marshall B. Tymn. St. Paul, MN: J. Colet Press.

Conceição, P., et al. (2020). *Human Development Report 2020. The Next Frontier: Human Development and the Anthropocene*. United Nations Development Programme, https://wfp.tind.io/record/60702?ln=en.

Condillac, Étienne Bonnot de (1754). *Traité des sensations*. Vol. I of *Œuvres philosophiques de Condillac*, 23 vols, pp. 221–33. London and Paris: De Bure l'aîné.

Cook, Clarence (1854). Letters on Art – No. IV. In Sarah Burns and John Davis, eds. (2009), *American Art to 1900: A Documentary*, pp. 307–9. Berkeley: University of California Press.

Cosgrove, Denis E. (1984). *Social Formation and Symbolic Landscape*. London: Croom Helm.

Cosgrove, Denis E. (2008). *Geography and Vision: Seeing, Imagining and Representing the World*. London: I. B. Taurus.

DeLue, Rachael Z. (2004). *George Innes and the Science of Landscape*. Chicago, IL: University of Chicago Press.

DeLue, Rachael Z. (2020). Shoreline Landscape and the Edges of Empire. In Richard Read and Kenneth Haltman, eds., *Colonization, Wilderness and Spaces Between: Nineteenth-Century Landscape Painting in Australia and the United States*, pp. 50–68. Chicago, IL: Terra Foundation for American Art.

deStefano, Daniel (2006). Nahant Rocks: Geology of an Island, https://daniel destefano.wordpress.com/2007/04/13/nahant-rocks-geology-of-an-island/.

Dixon, Robert (1986). *The Course of Empire: Neo-Classical Culture in New South Wales, 1788–1860*. Melbourne: Oxford University Press.

Dumitrescu, Marius (2017). Optical Illusion: A Perspective on the Sense of Sight in Early Modern Philosophical Thinking. *Agathos* 8(2), 47–56.

Dunlap, William (1969). *A History of the Rise and Progress of the Arts of Design in the United States*, repr. 2 vols. New York: Dover Publications.

Durand, Asher Brown (1854). Letters on Landscape Painting. In Sarah Burns and John Davis, eds. (2009), *American Art to 1900: A Documentary*, pp. 290–7. Berkeley: University of California Press.

Eagleman, David, interviewed by Andrew Anthony (2021). The Working of the Brain Resembles Drug Dealers in Albuquerque. *The Guardian*, June 12, www .theguardian.com/science/2021/jun/12/david-eagleman-the-working-of-the-brain-resembles-drug-dealers-in-albuquerque?CMP=Share_iOSApp_Other.

Emerson, Ralph Waldo (1836). Nature. In vol. 1 of Robert Spiller et al., eds. (1971), *Collected Works of Ralph Waldo Emerson*, 10 vols, pp. 1–45. Cambridge, MA: Harvard University Press.

Emerson, Ralph Waldo (1841). Circles. In vol. II of Robert Spiller et al., eds. (1979), *Collected Works of Ralph Waldo Emerson*, 10 vols, pp. 176–90. Cambridge, MA: Harvard University Press.

Emerson, Ralph Waldo (1844a). The Poet. In vol. III of Robert Spiller et al., eds. (1984), *Collected Works of Ralph Waldo Emerson*, 10 vols, pp. 1–24. Cambridge, MA: Harvard University Press.

Emerson, Ralph Waldo (1844b). The Young American. In vol. I of Robert Spiller et al., eds. (1971), *Collected Works of Ralph Waldo Emerson*, 10 vols, pp. 222–43. Cambridge, MA: Harvard University Press.

Emerson, Ralph Waldo (1939). *The Letters of Ralph Waldo Emerson*, ed. Ralph L. Rusk, 6 vols. New York: Columbia University Press.

Emerson, Ralph Waldo (1971–2013). *Collected Works of Ralph Waldo Emerson*, ed. Robert Spiller et al., 10 vols. Cambridge MA: Harvard University Press.

Fabricant, Carole (1987). The Literature of Domestic Tourism and the Public Consumption of Private Property. In Felicity Nussbaum and Laura Brown, eds., *The New Eighteenth Century: Theory, Politics. English Literature*, pp. 254–75. New York: Methuen.

Fearn, John (1812), *An Essay on Consciousness: Or a Series of Evidences of a Distinct Mind*, 2nd ed. London: Longman, Hurst, Rees et al.

Foley, Mary (1995–6). Ralph Waldo Emerson and the Gloucester Lyceum. *American Art Journal* 27(1–2), 99–101.

Foucault, Michel (1973). *The Birth of the Clinic: An Archaeology of Medical Perception*. New York: Random House.

Genesis 10: 9. Holy Bible: King James Version.

Georgi, Karen L. (2013). *Critical Shift: Rereading Jarves, Cook, Stillman and the Narratives of Nineteenth-Century American Art*. Philadelphia: Pennsylvania State University Press.

Gibson, James, J. (1951). What is a Form? *Psychological Review* 58(6), 403–12.

Gilpin, William (1782). *Observations on the River Wye, and several parts of South Wales, &c., relative chiefly to Picturesque Beauty; made In the Summer of the Year 1770*. London: Blamire in the Strand.

Gilpin, William (1794). *Three Essays on Picturesque Beauty; On Picturesque Travel and on Sketching Landscape, to which is added a poem, on Landscape Painting*. London: R. Blamire.

Glenney, Brian (2013a). Molyneux's Question. *Internet Encyclopedia of Philosophy*, https://iep.utm.edu/molyneux/.

Glenney, Brian (2013b). Philosophical Problems, Cluster Concepts and the Many Lives of Molyneux's Question. *Biology and Philosophy* 28(3), 541–58.

Glenney, Brian (2014). Perception and Prosopagnosia in Mark 8.22–26. *Journal for the Study of the New Testament* 37(1), 71–85.

Gooding, Janda (2007). The Politics of a Panorama: Robert Dale and King George Sound. In Norman Etherington, ed., *Mapping Colonial Conquest: Australia and Southern Africa*, pp. 66–78. Crawley: UWA Press.

Greenberg, Clement (1993). *Clement Greenberg, The Collected Essays and Criticism, Volume 4, Modernism with a Vengeance, 1957–1969*, ed. John O'Brian. Chicago, IL: University of Chicago Press.

Hamilakis, Yannis (2011). Archaeologies of the Senses. In Timothy Insoll, ed., *The Oxford Handbook of the Archaeology of Ritual and Religion*, pp. 208–25. Oxford: Oxford University Press.

Hatfield, Gary (2009). *Perception and Cognition: Essays in the Philosophy of Psychology*. Oxford: Clarendon Press.

Hazlitt, William (1812). *Lectures on English Philosophy.* In vol. II of P. P. Howe, ed., *The Complete Works of William Hazlitt*, 21 vols, pp. 121–284. London: J. M. Dent and Sons.

Hazlitt, William (1814a). Observations on Mr. Wordsworth's Poem *The Excursion.* In vol. IV of P. P. Howe, ed., *The Complete Works of William Hazlitt*, 21 vols., pp. 111–25. London: J. M. Dent and Sons.

Hazlitt, William (1814b). Wilson's Landscapes, at the British Institution. In vol. XVIII of P. P. Howe, ed., *The Complete Works of William Hazlitt*, 21 vols., pp. 24–8. London: J. M. Dent and Sons.

Hazlitt, William (1816). On *Gusto.* In vol. IV of P. P. Howe, ed., *The Complete Works of William Hazlitt*, 21 vols., pp. 77–80. London: J. M. Dent and Sons.

Hazlitt, William (1821). On a Landscape of Nicolas Poussin. In vol. VIII of P. P. Howe, ed., *The Complete Works of William Hazlitt*, 21 vols., pp. 168–74. London: J. M. Dent and Sons.

Hazlitt, William (1822a). On Going a Journey. In vol. VIII of P. P. Howe, ed., *The Complete Works of William Hazlitt*, 21 vols., pp. 181–9. London: J. M. Dent and Sons.

Hazlitt, William (1822b). Why Distant Objects Please. In vol. VIII of P. P. Howe, ed., *The Complete Works of William Hazlitt*, 21 vols., pp. 255–64. London: J. M. Dent and Sons.

Hazlitt, William (1822c). On Milton's Sonnets. In vol. VIII of P. P. Howe, ed., *The Complete Works of William Hazlitt*, 21 vols., pp. 174–81. London: J. M. Dent and Sons.

Hazlitt, William (1823). The Dulwich Gallery. In vol. X of P. P. Howe, ed., *The Complete Works of William Hazlitt*, 21 vols., pp. 17–26. London: J. M. Dent and Sons.

Hazlitt, William (1930–4). *The Complete Works of William Hazlitt*, ed. P. P. Howe, 21 vols. London: J. M. Dent and Sons.

Held, Richard, Yuri Ostrovsky, Beatrice de Gelder, et al. (2011). The Newly Sighted Fail to Match Seen with Felt. *Nature Neuroscience* 14, 551–3, https://doi.org.ezproxy.library.uwa.edu.au/10.1038/nn.2.

Hirschberg, Julius (1985). Vol. II of *The History of Ophthalmology*, trans. F. C. Blodi, 11 vols. Bonn: Verlag.

Hodder, Alan. D. (1989). *Emerson's Rhetoric of Revelation:* Nature, *the Reader, and the Apocalyptic Vision.* University Park: Pennsylvania State University Press.

Holdsworth, Sam (n.d.). *Brace's Rock Series. Fitz Henry Lane Online*, Cape Ann Museum, http://fitzhenrylaneonline.org/essays/index.php?name=Braces_Rock_Series.

Hughes-Warrington, Marnie, and Ian Tregenza (2008). State and Civilization in Australian New Idealism, 1890–1950. *History of Political Thought* 29(1), 89–108.

Humboldt, Alexander von (1795). Über Denken und Sprechen. Vol. VII of Albert Leitzmann et al., eds. (1903–37). *Gesammelte Schriften*, 17 vols, pp. 581–3. Berlin: B. Behr.

Humboldt, Alexander von (1848–52). *Cosmos: A Sketch of a Physical Description of the Universe*, trans. E. C. Otté, 5 vols. London: Henry G. Bohn.

Isiah, 40: 12, 16. Holy Bible: King James Version.

Johnson, Jessica P. (2020). Molyneux's Problem: Blind Philosophy. *BrainFacts.org*, www.brainfacts.org/thinking-sensing-and-behaving/vision/2020/molyneuxs-problem-blind-philosophy-032620.

Jones, David (2005). In Conversation with Bruno Latour: Historiography of 'Science in Action', https://dspace.mit.edu/bitstream/handle/1721.1/103818/sts-310-fall-2005/contents/assignments/paper2.pdf.

Jordens, Ann-Mari (1979). *The Stenhouse Circle: Literary Life in Mid-Nineteenth Century Sydney*. Melbourne: Melbourne University Press.

Kepler, Johannes (1604). *Ad Vitellionem Paralipomena, quibus astronomiæ pars optica traditur*. Frankfurt: Claudium Marnium et Hæredes Ioannis Aubrii.

Kusserow, K. (2018a). Ordering the Land. In Karl Kusserow and Alan C. Braddock, eds., *Nature's Nation: American Art and Environment*, pp. 71–101. New Haven: Yale University Press.

Kusserow, K. (2018b). The Trouble with Empire. In Karl Kusserow and Alan C. Braddock, eds., *Nature's Nation: American Art and Environment*, pp. 103–39. New Haven: Yale University Press.

Land, Michael F., and Dan-Eric Nilsson (2012). *Animal Eyes*. 2nd ed. Oxford: Oxford University Press.

Leffler, Christopher T., Stephen G. Schwartz, Eric Peterson, et al. (2021). The First Cataract Surgeons in the British Isles. *American Journal of Opthalmology* 230, 75–122.

Leibniz, G. W. (1981). *New Essays Concerning Human Understanding*, trans. Peter Remnant and Jonathan Bennett. Cambridge: Cambridge University Press.

Lessing, Gotthold Ephraim (1836). *Laocoon: Or, The Limits of Poetry and Painting*, trans. William Ross. London: Ridgeway.

Locke, John (1689). *Two Treatises of Government*, 1823 edn. In Paul E. Sigmund (2005), *The Selected Political Writings of John Locke*, pp. 3–125. New York: W. W. Norton.

Locke, John (1975). *An Essay Concerning Human Understanding*, 1700 edn., ed. Peter H. Nidditch. Oxford: Clarendon Press.

Makin, Simon (2019). Four Technologies that Could Transform the Treatment of Blindness. *Nature Outlook: The Eye*, www.nature.com/articles/d41586-019-01107-8/.

Manthorne, Katherine Emma (1989). *Tropical Renaissance: North American Artists Exploring Latin America, 1839–1879*. Washington, DC: Smithsonian.

Mark, 8: 22–6. Holy Bible, King James Version.

Marsh, George Perkins (1860). The Study of Nature. *Christian Examiner* 68(1), 33–62.

Marx, Leo (2000). *The Machine in the Garden: Technology and the Pastoral Ideal in America*. Oxford: Oxford University Press.

Matthen, Mohan, and Jonathan Cohen (2020). Many Molyneux Questions. *Australasian Journal of Philosophy* 98(1), 47–63.

Merleau-Ponty, Maurice (2002). *Phenomenology of Perception*, trans. Colin Smith. London: Routledge.

Miller, Angela L. (1993). *The Empire of the Eye: Landscape Representation and American Cultural Politics, 1825–1875*. Ithaca, NY: Cornell University Press.

Miller, Angela L. (2001). Albert Bierstadt, Landscape Aesthetics and the Meanings of the West in the Civil War Era. *Art Institute of Chicago Museum Studies* 27(1), 40–59, 101–2.

Miller, Perry (1956). *Errand into the Wilderness*. Cambridge, MA: Belknap Press of Harvard University Press.

Milnes, Tim (2000). Seeing in the Dark: Hazlitt's Immanent Idealism. *Studies in Romanticism* 39(1), 3–25.

Milnes, Tim (2019). *The Testimony of the Sense: Empiricism and the Essay from Hume to Hazlitt*. Oxford: Oxford University Press.

Milton, John (2005). *Paradise Lost*. Oxford: Oxford University Press, https://ebookcentral-proquest-com.ezproxy.library.uwa.edu.au/lib/uwa/reader.action?docID=422470.

Monks, Sarah (2018). Introduction. In Katherine M. Bourguignon and Peter John Brownlee, eds., *Conversations with the Collection: A Terra Foundation Collection Handbook*, pp. 16–26. Chicago, IL: Terra Foundation for American Art.

Morgan, Michael J. (1977). *Molyneux's Question: Vision, Touch, and the Philosophy of Perception*. Cambridge: Cambridge University Press.

Muir, John (1894). *The Mountains of California*. New York: The Century Co., https://vault.sierraclub.org/john_muir_exhibit/writings/the_mountains_of_california/chapter_4.aspx.

O'Donnell, C. Oliver (2017). Depicting Berkeleyan Idealism: A Study of Two Portraits by John Smibert. *Word & Image: A Journal of Visual-Verbal Enquiry* 33(1), 18–34.

OED. *Oxford English Dictionary*, online version, www.oed.com/.

Ott, Walter (2020). Locke on the Role of Judgment in Perception. *European Journal of Philosophy* 28 (3), 670–84.

Paley, William (1815). *Natural Theology; Or Evidences of the Existence and Attributes of The Deity, collected from the appearances of nature*, 15th ed. London: F. C. and J. Rivington et al.

Panofsky, Erwin (1991). *Perspective as Symbolic Form*. New York: Zone Books.

Parry III, Ellwood C. (2001). Cooper, Cole and the Last of the Mohicans. In Mary Louise Krumrine and Susan Clare Scott, eds., *Art and the Native American: Perceptions, Reality and Influences*, pp. 146–95. University Park: The Pennsylvania State University Press.

Pastore, Nicholas (1971). *Selective History of the Theories of Perception, 1650–1950*. Oxford: Oxford University Press.

Paterson, Mark (2006). Seeing with the Hands, Touching with the Eyes: Vision, Touch and the Enlightenment Spatial Imaginary. *The Senses and Society*, 1 (2), published online 16 April 2015, www.tandfonline.com/doi/abs/10.2752/174589206778055538.

Paulin, Tom (1998). *The Day-Star of Liberty: William Hazlitt's Radical Style*. London, Faber and Faber.

Pfister, Wally, dir. (2014). *Transcendence*. Warner Brothers.

Plato, *The Timaeus* (c.360 BC). Perseus Digital Library, Tufts, www.perseus.tufts.edu/hopper/text?doc=Perseus%3Atext%3A1999.01.0180%3Atext%3DTim.%3Asection%3D17a.

Pullin, Ruth (2020). The Düsseldorf Effect: Nineteenth-Century Practice with Twenty-First-Century Relevance. In Richard Read and Kenneth Haltman, eds., *Colonization, Wilderness and Spaces Between: Nineteenth-Century Landscape Painting in Australia and the United States*, pp. 88–122. Chicago, IL: Terra Foundation for American Art.

Purdy, Jedediah (2015). *After Nature: A Politics for the Anthropocene*. Cambridge, MA: Harvard University Press.

Quilley, Geoff (2004). William Hodges, Artist of Empire. In John Bonehill and Geoff Quilley, eds., *William Hodges, 1744–1797: The Art of Exploration*, pp. 1–7. New Haven, CT: Yale University Press.

Raab, Jennifer (2015). *Frederick Church: The Art and Science of Detail*. New Haven, CT: Yale University Press.

Raab, Jennifer (2018). Catalogue Entry. In Tim Barringer, Gillian Forrester, Sophie Lynford, Jennifer Raab, and Nicholas Robbins, *Picturesque and*

Sublime: Thomas Cole's Trans-Atlantic Inheritance, pp. 152–30. New Haven, CT: Yale University Press.

Read, Richard (2020). Perception, History, and Geology: The Heritage of Molyneux's Question in Colonial Landscape Painting. In Richard Read and Kenneth Haltman, eds., *Colonization, Wilderness and Spaces Between: Nineteenth-Century Landscape Painting in Australia and the United States*, pp. 124–44. Chicago, IL: Terra Foundation for American Art.

Riskin, Jessica (2002). *Science in the Age of Sensibility: The Sentimental Empiricists of the French Enlightenment*. Chicago, IL: University of Chicago Press.

Rudwick. Martin J. S. (1976). The Emergence of a Visual Language for Geological Science, 1760–1840. *History of Science* 14, 149–95.

Ruskin, John (1843). *Modern Painters I*. Vol. V of E. T. Cook and Alexander Wedderburn, eds., *The Works of John Ruskin*. Library ed., 39 vols. London: George Allen.

Ruskin, John (1851). *The Stones of Venice I*. Vol. IX of E. T. Cook and Alexander Wedderburn, eds. (1903–12). *The Works of John Ruskin*, Library ed., 39 vols. London: George Allen.

Ruskin, John (1857). *Elements of Drawing*. Vol. XV of E. T. Cook and Alexander Wedderburn, eds. (1903–12). *The Works of John Ruskin*, pp. 1–288. Library ed., 39 vols. London: George Allen.

Ruskin, John (1851). *Praeterita*. Vol. XXXV of E. T. Cook and Alexander Wedderburn, eds. (1903–12). *The Works of John Ruskin*, Library ed., 39 vols. London: George Allen.

Ruskin, John (1903–12). *The Works of John Ruskin*. Library ed., ed. E. T. Cook and Alexander Wedderburn, 39 vols. London: George Unwin.

Sassen, Brigitte (2004). Kant on Molyneux's Problem. *British Journal for the History of Philosophy*, 12(3), 471–85.

Scott, Michael (2010). William Hazlitt and Ralph Waldo Emerson: Unitarianism, the Museum, and the Aesthetics of Power. *Wordsworth Circle* 41(2), 93–103.

Scruton, Roger (2001). *Kant: A Very Short Introduction*. Oxford: Oxford University Press.

Smith, Bernard (1960). *European Vision and the South Pacific, 1768–1850: A Study in the History of Art and Ideas*. Oxford: Oxford University Press.

Stein, Roger B. (1967). *John Ruskin and Aesthetic Thought in America, 1840–1900*. Cambridge, MA: Harvard University Press.

Straker, Stephen (1976). The Eye Made 'Other': Dürer, Kepler, and the Mechanization of Light and Vision. In L. A. Knafla, M. S. Staum and T. H. E. Travers, eds., *Science, Technology and Culture in Perspective*, pp. 7–24. Calgary: University of Calgary.

Stula, Nancy (2008). *At Home and Abroad: The Transcendental Landscape of Christopher Pearse Cranch (1813–1893)*. New London, CT: Lyman Allyn Art Museum.

Szécsényi, Endre (2017). The Regard of the First Man: On Joseph Addison's Aesthetic Categories. *History of European Ideas* 43(6), 582–97.

Thomson, James (1981). *The Seasons*, ed. James Sambrook. Oxford: Clarendon Press.

Tobin, Beth Fowles (1999). *Picturing Imperial Power: Colonial Subjects in Eighteenth-Century British Painting*. Durham, NC: Duke University Press.

Turner, Frederick Jackson (2008). *The Significance of the Frontier in American History*. London: Penguin.

Turner, R. Steven (1993). Consensus and Controversy: Helmholtz on the Visual Perception of Space. In David Cahan, ed., *Hermann von Helmholtz and the Foundations of Nineteenth-Century Science*, pp. 154–203. Berkeley: University of California Press.

Turner, Tom (1956). *Turners of Augusta*. Perth, WA: Paterson Brokensha Pty.

Van Cleve, James (2007). Reid's Answer to Molyneux's Question. *The Monist* 90(2), 251–70.

Van Den Berg, Sara (2009). Full Sight, Fancied Sight, and Touch: Milton's Sonnet 23 and Molyneux's Question. *Ben Jonson Journal* 16(1–2), 16–32.

Veith, Gene Edward (2001). *Painters of Faith: The Spiritual Landscape in Nineteenth-Century America*. Washington, DC: Regnery Publishing, Inc.

Wade, Nicholas J. (2005). *Perception and Illusion: Historical Perspectives*. New York: Springer.

Wallach, Alan (2002). Thomas Cole's 'River in the Catskills' as Antipastoral. *Art Bulletin* 84(2), 334–50.

Walls, Laura Dassow (2003). *Emerson's Life in Science: The Culture of Truth*. Ithaca, NY: Cornell University Press.

Walker, John (1837). *The Philosophy of the Eye: Being a Familiar Exposition of its Mechanism, and of the Phenomenon of Vision, With a View to Evidence of Design*. London: C. Knight.

Welleck, René (1931). *Immanuel Kant in England, 1793–1838*. Princeton, NJ: Princeton University Press.

Williams, Michael (2010). Clearing the Forests. In Michael P. Conzen, ed., *The Making of the American Landscape*, pp. 162–87. New York: Routledge.

Wimsatt, W. K. Jr (1948). *Philosophic Words: A Study of Style and Meaning in the 'Rambler' and 'Dictionary' of Samuel Johnson*. New Haven, CT: Yale University Press.

Winckles, Andrew (2010). Locke and Addison's 'Pleasures of the Imagination'. In *18th Century Religion, Literature, and Culture: Explanations of Cultural Intersections*, https://18thcenturyculture.wordpress.com/2010/10/04/locke-and-addisons-pleasures-of-the-imagination/.

Wolf, Brian (1982). Revolution in Landscape: John Trumbull and Picturesque Painting. In Helen A. Cooper, ed., *John Trumbull: the Hand and Spirit of a Painter*, pp. 206–22. Cambridge and New York: Yale University Press.

Woodward, Jamie (2014). *The Ice Age: A Very Short Introduction*. Oxford: Oxford University Press.

Wordsworth, William (1961). *The Poetical Works of Wordsworth*, ed. Thomas Hutchinson and Ernest De Selincourt. London: Oxford University Press.

Yussof, Kathryn (2020). Geologics: Natural Resources as Necropolitics. Online lecture, Harvard University Graduate School of Design, www.youtube.com/watch?v=QM8B-XZG8OQ.

Cambridge Elements ☰

Histories of Emotions and the Senses

Jan Plamper
University of Limerick

Jan Plamper is Professor of History at the University of Limerick. His publications include *The History of Emotions: An Introduction* (Oxford University Press, 2015); a multidisciplinary volume on fear; and articles on the sensory history of the Russian Revolution and on the history of soldiers' fears in World War One. He has also authored *The Stalin Cult: A Study in the Alchemy of Power* (Yale University Press, 2012) and *Das neue Wir: Warum Migration dazugehört. Eine andere Geschichte der Deutschen* (S. Fischer, 2019).

About the Series

Born of the emotional and sensory 'turns', *Elements in Histories of Emotions and the Senses* move one of the fastest-growing interdisciplinary fields forward. The series is aimed at scholars across the humanities, social sciences, and life sciences, embracing insights from a diverse range of disciplines, from neuroscience to art history and economics. Chronologically and regionally broad, encompassing global, transnational, and deep history, it concerns such topics as affect theory, intersensoriality, embodiment, human-animal relations, and distributed cognition.

Cambridge Elements ≡

Histories of Emotions and the Senses

A full series listing is available at: www.cambridge.org/EHES

Printed in the United States
by Baker & Taylor Publisher Services